How to Kitesurf

Shawn Tieskotter

Sign up at HowToKitesurf.com to access FREE video tutorials, discounts on gear and more!

Copyright © 2012
Shawn Tieskotter
All rights reserved.

ISBN: 978-0-9888996-1-2

Thank you for purchasing this book!

"Surfing soothes me, it's always been a kind of Zen experience for me. The ocean is so magnificent, peaceful, and awesome. The rest of the world disappears for me when I'm on a wave."
~ Paul Walker

Preface
Why Write a Book on Kiting?

I'm an avid kiter and an instructor. In the years I've been kiting, I've seen amazing athletes raise this sport to the level of an art form. I've also seen some serious accidents that could have been avoided. I love this sport and want to see it grow, so I have three main reasons for writing this book:

- I want to help new kiters get a safe start and be able to learn all the important facts about kiting.

- I am committed to doing all I can to assure the safety of my fellow kiters, both beginners and the experts they share kiting sites with.

- I mean to do all that I can to assure the existing kiting sites remain open to us. Avoidable accidents give the sport a bad name and if it is perceived as dangerous or too reckless, we'll get banned and we all lose out.

Throughout this book, you'll find some special pointers from my friend Tyson Sullivan, who is also a certified kiting instructor and a very experienced rider. They will be noted, naturally, as **"Tips from Tyson."**

Disclaimer

Kiteboarding is an extreme sport and participation could result in serious bodily injury or death, not only to participants but also anyone in the area.

While this book is intended to provide information on equipment and techniques and to make safety a priority for kiters, it is in no way to be used as a replacement for lessons and instruction in proper use of equipment. Each manufacturer will provide instructions for safe equipment usage and they should be followed carefully.

The author and publisher are not responsible for any loss or accident resulting from the use or misuse of the material herein.

Table of Contents

Chapter 1: What Am I Getting Myself Into? 3
  An Overview of Kiteboarding 3
  Why Take Up Kiting? 7
    Can Anybody Do It? 8
    How About Women? 9
  Chapter 1 FAQs & Common Misconceptions 10

Chapter 2: Getting Started with Kiting 11
  Trainer Kites 15
  Kiting Equipment 17
    The Kite 17
    Boards 21
    The Harness 23
    The Control Bar 24
  Chapter 2 FAQs & Common Misconceptions 26

Chapter 3: Safety 28
  The Kiting Environment: What Makes for a Safe Place to Kite? 28
    Safety Rule #1: Know Your Wind 30
    And Only Go Out When You Know It Is Safe 30
    The Weather 37
  Sharing Space: Who Has the Right of Way? 40
    Right of Way with Other Kiters 41
  Communication: Vocabulary and Hand Signals 45
  Safety Equipment 53
  Kitemares 54
  Chapter 3 FAQs & Common Misconceptions 56

International Right of Way Rules 57

Chapter 4: Equipment Operation 58
  Visualization 58
  Setting Up & Practicing with a Trainer Kite 58
    Launching the Trainer Kite 62
    Controlling the Trainer Kite 63
  Know Your Equipment 70
    The Package 70
    The Kite 71
    Bridle Options 72
  Stock Setting 73
  Upwind Setting 73
  Downwind Setting 74
  "Boss" & "Big Mama" Bridles 74
    Single Line Setups 74
  Rigging Tips 76
  Carrot Bar Equipment Diagram 79

    Carrot Bar Stock Set-Up 81
    Carrot Bar: Suicide Connection Set-Up 82
    Carrot Bar: Double Depower Set-Up 84
    Carrot Bar: School Safety Set-Up 87
    Carrot Bar: One Release Set-Up 90
    The Quick Release & Safety Leash 91
  Tips & Info 93
  Chapter 4 FAQs & Common Misconceptions 97

Chapter 5: Techniques 98
  Assisted Landing 101
  Self-Launch 101
  Self-Landing 103
  Relaunching 103
    How to Perform a Rabbit Relaunch 104
    How to Perform a Traditional Relaunch 106
  Body Dragging 108
  Getting Up on the Board 108
  Self-Rescue 109
    How to Recover Your Kite 110
    Self-Rescue in Onshore or Side Onshore Winds 111
    How to Perform a Self-Rescue 112
  Avoid Getting Lofted 116
  Riding Upwind 117
  Chapter 5 FAQs & Common Misconceptions 120

Chapter 6: Buying Gear 121
  New vs. Used Equipment 121
  Shops vs. Dealers 122
  Forums 122
  Professional Riders 122

Conclusion 124

About the Author 126

Chapter 1:
What Am I Getting Myself Into?

An Overview of Kiteboarding

Kiteboarding is an extreme sport that consists of boarding (on water, sand, or snow) while being propelled by a very large kite. The kite is solely under the control of the boarder and no boats, planes, elevated structures, or any other vehicle or specialized location is required. The sport is also called "kite surfing" and, less commonly, "fly surfing."

Kiting is a relatively new sport, but it has become much more popular in the last few years. There are somewhere between 150,000 and 200,000 kite surfers around the globe now, and the sport gets easier and safer all the time. With the increasing popularity of the sport, the equipment is constantly being improved and better techniques are being developed.

There are several different kinds of kiteboarding:

Kiteboarding (on water) — Kiteboarding is the most popular kind and is done all over the world. The board used is similar to a wakeboard or snowboard, and the kiter straps his or her feet onto it. Movement through the water is controlled by the feet, while the kite is controlled by a bar that is held in the hands. This is sometimes also called "kite surfing."

Kite surfing (with a surfboard) — Kite surfing is a specific kind of kiting, although the term is sometimes used to mean any kind of kiteboarding. A special short, wide surfboard with multiple fins is preferable for this kind of kite surfing, and the actual surfing looks very similar to regular surfing. The difference is that the kiter uses his kite to propel him through the water to get set up for the wave and to gain momentum for catching waves.

Snow kiting — Of course, takes place on snow and can be done in any place with enough snow and wide open spaces. The board and footwork are both similar to those used in snowboarding, but the kite allows you to get out and play without having to pay for a lift ticket or even have a mountain for that matter. You can kite on flat ground and have just as much or more fun since you can focus on your skills rather than always watch for environmental hazards.

Land boarding — If you have a wide open area of sand, you can kiteboard there. There are some advantages to land boarding, like accessibility in regions that don't have water available, and you don't have to know how to swim. Falling on land is different than falling in water, though, so there are some special precautions associated with land boarding too.

Why Take Up Kiting?

Kiteboarding isn't for everyone, but it is a lot of fun and one of the most accessible of extreme sports. Minimal equipment is required and there is a way to do it in most regions, whether you have beaches, lakes, or just plains.

Wakeboarders – Unless you have your own boat with an on-call captain, you will love the freedom of kiteboarding. You can go out whenever you want to and don't even have to pay for gas. There are even fewer restrictions for when you can go out because you don't have to worry about choppy water and wind. Wakeboarders are also perfectly set up to start kiteboarding because they have the footwork aspect taken care of. Once you get that down, you're halfway there. All you have to do is build on your already established skills

Snowboarders – No lift ticket required! Kiting only requires a wide-open, snow-covered surface, a board, a kite, and, of course, some wind. With a kite, you can even go uphill.

Windsurfers – Less wind is required, and you can do big jumps even if the water is totally flat. The equipment is immensely easier to haul around: a couple of kites and a (much shorter) board and you are good to go.*

Surfers – All that time that you spend waiting for a good set and then paddling out trying to catch the right wave can be spent on the board with a kite. You can still ride the waves; you just aren't limited by them.

Skate/Mountain-boarders – In kiting, mountain boards are called "landboards," and those big inflated tires work great on hard-packed dirt, sand, and grass. With a kite, you don't have to get to the top of a hill to get some action. Any wide-open field or a beach gives you a place to cruise or fly. You get to choose!

Skimboarders – If you love the sensation of cruising along the water's edge, just think how free you'll feel when you don't have to run to get your momentum, and gravity doesn't control the length of your ride!

Non-boarders – Don't feel left out. If you don't do any kind of boarding, you're going to need to learn wakeboarding skills. You need to get this part down before adding a kite, or it will be just too much to learn all at one time. But, don't be discouraged. You can start practicing with a trainer kite on land during the time you are building your board skills, and soon you'll be ready for kiting.

> ***Special note for windsurfers:** The way you handle the board in kiteboarding is very different than it is in windsurfing. You will need to do some wakeboarding before you are ready to go kiteboarding.

Can Anybody Do It?

Quite frankly, no. Kiteboarding is an active sport and while you don't have to be an athlete to enjoy it, you do need to be in fairly good shape and strong enough to handle your equipment in some fairly strong winds. However, don't worry about needing to have a huge amount of upper body strength. The harness system uses your body weight to hold the kite, and your arms only control it (unless you are unhooked to do really advanced tricks like flips). Beginners do get bounced around and roughed up a bit, so you have to be able to take a fall and handle some physical discomfort.

How About Women?

Kiting requires a basic level of fitness but as with men, any woman who is in reasonably good shape has the potential to be a kiter if she can manage the physical exertion and take the occasional poundings that come with skating, snowboarding, or surfing.

Chapter 1 FAQs & Common Misconceptions

Q: I've been checking out kitesurfing videos online, and those guys all look like they are in their 20s. I'm over 40. Is that "over the hill" for this sport?

A: Not at all! In kiteboarding, like most other outdoor sports, the really extreme tricks are usually being done by the more aggressive, younger set. Most people who kite aren't concerned with aerial flips or any of the other wild and crazy stunts; they just want to get out and have fun. In fact, I have personally seen kids as young as 5 years old learning the sport and guys 72 years young going out every day that there's a good wind. Kiting is fast and fun at all ability levels.

Q: Kiteboarding looks like a lot of fun, but I've got a family depending on me. Am I going to break my neck if I get out there on a kite?

A: The whole point of this book is to teach the basics and give you a reference so you can always be sure you are kiting safely. Kiting is something that a lot of families, including young kids, enjoy together. You have a lot of control over your safety in choosing the equipment you buy and determining what conditions you go out in.

Chapter 2:
Getting Started with Kiting

The Adventure Begins...With a Lesson

Sports enthusiasts love to dive right in and start having fun. It's only natural, but in this sport you really do need to start with a lesson or two. Sure, a buddy on the beach can show you the equipment and tell you what to do, but a lesson is structured to cover all the basics you need to know to get a safe start.

There are two kinds of lessons that can be combined into one day. Ground school is where you start. Before you start handling equipment, you'll need to know when and where it's safe to use it, how to safely set everything up, how to use the signals that kiters are expected to use, and, especially, the basics of working with the wind. These are all the concepts we'll be covering in this book, which you can refer back to any time you need to.

Remember to Have Fun and Be SAFE!

2: Getting Started with Kiting | 13

After you learn the ground school basics, it's really important that you have a qualified instructor take you out the first time you actually launch a kite. Remember, you can't control the wind and even though there are a lot of factors that you can monitor, it takes some experience to know how to deal with the unexpected, so don't risk going out solo for your initial venture with a kite.

Professional lessons will teach you:

- When it's safe to kite
- Where it's safe to kite
- What kind of equipment you need
- What to look for in equipment
- What is – and how to use – a trainer kite
- How to operate your equipment
- Basic techniques
- Differences between the various kinds of kiting
- Special procedures and communication signals
- How to read the wind
- What kind of winds you can kite in and which to avoid
- What to do when the unexpected happens
- How to help another kiter in a crisis

By taking an in-person lesson with a local expert, you will also learn:

- Local sources for equipment
- Where you can kite safely in your area
- Unique hazards and conditions in your area
- Local groups and organizations where you can connect with other kiters
- Characteristics of particular equipment. The instructor's equipment provides a try-before-you-buy opportunity to make sure you know what you need.

Before you even go for your first lesson, I'd like to make a rather unusual recommendation. Go online and do a search for kiteboarding accidents. I don't want to scare you off. I want to give you an opportunity to see for yourself just how many things can go wrong and the seriousness of the results so that you really get how important it is for you to get a good handle on the basics and safety procedures of this exciting sport.

When you read stories and watch videos about kiting accidents, you will notice two things that recur throughout. One is that accidents happen to beginners and experts alike. As people get more skilled they get more confident, and sometimes over-confidence leads them to break rules that get them into trouble.

Another is that people will often talk about their own accidents and injuries because they want to help other people avoid the same situation. You'll also notice that they are usually talking about what they'll do differently next time. Kiters tend to be passionate about the sport and don't like to give it up.

There is a lot of information in this book. It's a great idea to read through it before you get started to give yourself some familiarity with the equipment, procedures, and jargon of kiting. It would also be good to read through it after a lesson to reinforce what you've learned – and then again after you've gotten some practice – because it will have a lot more meaning to you.

If you do some kiting and take a break from it or are only able to participate when on vacation, etc., be sure to review the terms and techniques before you get back out there. Even kinesthetic learners (those who learn best by doing) will benefit from getting a handle on the vocabulary and practices in the book.

Trainer Kites

Before you start using a kite that will move your body, you need to start out with a smaller, easy-to-manage kite so you can learn how to control it without placing yourself or others at risk of a collision. An instructor will always start you off working with a trainer kite, and it is recommended that you buy one so you can get a lot of practice.

Trainer kites are designed to be released if you get in trouble, and the kite will simply depower and float in the wind instead of having any pull. Trainers are much smaller than regular kites and are usually 1 to 3 meters. (Regular kites for adults typically range from 7 to 23 meters.)

This book will explain how kites work in the wind, but you will need to get a lot of practice before you are proficient at handling a kite. A trainer makes it easy to get started and to bail out and restart when something doesn't work out.

Trainer kites also let you get out and play without having a lot of equipment to hook up. They are easy to launch and provide a great opportunity to get a feel for

various types of winds.

When purchasing a trainer kite, you can go very basic. There are models that cost up to $500, but you don't need to invest that much in a trainer. You need something that will let you get a feel for the wind and learn the maneuvers that you will be using.

For an adult, a full 3-meter trainer kite is recommended because the 2-meter kite can whip around too much for you to really get a feel for the full power of the wind and the kite. However, you don't need an inflatable, and you don't need to get fancy with a 3- or 5-line kite. Just get a basic 2-line trainer, and use the money you save for better equipment when you buy a full-sized kite.

Get access to the best trainer kite on the market and take advantage of our bonuses!

HowToKitesurf.com

Kiting Equipment

Your equipment for kiting will consist of a kite, harness and bar, a board appropriate to whichever kind of kiting you are doing, and some basic safety equipment.

The Kite

Your kite is the piece of equipment that makes this sport what it is. The kite catches wind and translates that force into enough power to pull or lift your body and even to make it fly. There are two types of kites: foils and inflatables. There are also several different kinds of kites within those categories, but a few characteristics are consistent among all of them.

The size and shape of the kite determines how it will catch the wind, how much force it will have, and how responsive it will be to you. The edge of the kite that is at the top or toward you when it is in flight is called the leading edge. The lower – or far – edge is called the trailing edge. The ends of the kite are called wingtips.

Some kites have a system of cords and pulleys that are part of the kite. These are called bridles. You control the kite by lines that attach either directly to the kite or to

You can secure your kite by putting your board on the leading edge.

the bridles.

Inflatables

An inflatable kite is made of ripstop nylon with an inflatable tube across the leading edge and shorter tubes (struts) that run from the leading edge to the trailing edge. Some kites have multiple valves for filling each tube separately, and some kites have all the tubes connected, so you can pump them up from one place.

Use the supplied pump for filling your kite. You don't want to blow air into the kite by mouth because your breath contains a lot of moisture that can be difficult to get out of the tubes.

Be sure to check manufacturer instructions for properly filling your kite. There may also be valves to close off each section after it is filled, so if you get a puncture your kite won't fully deflate. If you have them, be sure to close them off properly.

The inflated tubes help to form the shape of the kite. In flight, the kite always has some degree of an arched shape that can range from gently curving to a deep "C" shape. It is the shape in flight that gives each style of kite its unique characteristics. The arch also makes water re-launching much easier, which accounts for the popularity of inflatables. There are four basic shapes of inflatable kites. Deltas and hybrids are subsets of bow kites with specific characteristics:

◊◊◊ Tips From Tyson ◊◊◊

Kite manufacturers often underrate the proper pressure needed to get optimum performance. An underinflated kite can be dangerous, especially in strong winds. Any modern kite should be pumped quite hard—typically, 10 psi should cut it. This is especially true for race-style kites. They need to be rock solid!

◊◊◊

Pumping up the kite

C-kites: When laid out flat, a C-kite is generally rectangular, with the leading and trailing edges both being convex curves. When it is in the air, it forms a high C-shaped arch. This is the original kite design for kiteboarding, and the lines attach directly to the four corners of the kite without bridles. C-kites are agile and quick turning, but can be difficult for beginners to handle.

Bow Kites: In the air, a bow kite (as in "bow and arrow") looks similar to a C-kite but has a flattened profile at the top. Bridles on the leading edge attach to the lines and when the control bar is released, the kite depowers immediately, making it safer than a C kite for beginners. The bow kite has a concave trailing edge when laid out flat.

Delta Kites: When viewed from above, a delta kite's leading edge sweeps back to the wingtips, giving it a more triangular shape than the other kites have. The delta kite has bridles on the leading edge and is a type of bow kite or a hybrid but has a shorter, fatter shape that gives it distinct flight characteristics. One of the best for beginners is that it is easy to re-launch, and you can feel the power rising slowly rather than the sudden power up that you experience with C-kites.

Hybrids: In an effort to combine the benefits of the C-kite's quick turning and the bow kite's quick depower, designers have been experimenting with combining elements of the two designs. The resulting hybrids have some of the qualities of each, depending on just how they are designed.

Foils

These kites consist of two layers, and air flows between them through an opening that runs along the front edge. Inside the kite baffles form compartments, or cells, that permit air to flow between them and allow the kite to fill evenly. The shape of the baffles provides the airfoil/aerofoil shape of the kite, like the wing of a plane. It is this shape that causes the kite to lift as air flows more swiftly over the top of the foil.

Classic Foils: The cells in a classic foil are open so if it falls in the water, it gets wet inside and can't be re-launched. Classic foils are great trainer kites and work well for landboarding and snowkiting.

Valved Foils: Foil kites have been designed with valves that let air flow in and fill the kite but then do not let the air back out. These one-way valves allow foil kites to hold their air in the water so that they can be re-launched.

Boards

The board helps you stay on the surface of the water and move smoothly across the snow, sand, water, etc. You also use the board to control your direction.

There are several different kinds of kiteboards, and the one you want depends on the kind of riding you want to do, your skill level, and your size. First off, there are boards for water and snow and even boards with inflatable wheels for landboarding.

Boards designed for kitesurfing are designed to stick to the water, to be controllable, and to be able to "edge" (or dig into the water for control). They are also designed to be flexible so the rider isn't jarred while riding. However, all kitesurfing boards are not the same, and it's important to know what you're looking for before you buy.

One characteristic you will hear about is "rocker," which refers to the curvature in the shape of the board when viewed in profile from nose to tail. Wakeboards have a lot of rocker, but a kitesurfing board has a flatter mid-section to allow the edges to dig into the water. Different designs have varying degrees of rocker towards both tips.

If you look down the length of the board, you will probably see that the shape of the bottom from side to side is concave (they usually are). This concave shape helps the board stick to the water and also helps with edging. The major types of boards for kiteboarding on water are twintips, surfs, and skims.

Twintips are by far the most common and are very similar to wakeboards. They are identical at both ends, making them bi-directional in the water so that you can change your direction without turning the board around. Twintips are very versatile and are the best beginner board.

The boards will have foot pads, foot straps, a center handle, and fins. Your foot pads are where you connect to the board, so make sure they are cushy and the straps are adjustable. Those factors will affect your comfort every time you ride, which has a big impact on how long you can ride. Both foot pads and straps are ergonomically designed and should feel good.

Surfs are used for kiteboarding in waves and are styled similarly to surfboards, with a distinct nose and tail and skegs on the bottom. They are larger than twintips and have more flotation, which lets the rider use a smaller kite. Wave surfing requires quick directional changes, so fast turns of the kite and board are needed. Surfs may have a grip pad or pattern of grips and come with removable straps. Experienced surfers are used to moving their feet on the board so once the kite is integrated, the straps are usually not used.

Skims are thin, flat boards that are designed for use in shallow water. They have become a popular alternative for kiting on low-wind days because of their low-drag quality. Skimboards don't have straps, either, so are not the first choice for beginners. People who skim without a kite enjoy the added versatility of kiting, but skims are also a good choice for a second board to use when there just isn't quite enough wind to ride your twintip.

When you choose a board, you need to consider your skill, size, and style. Bigger boards are more stable and, therefore, are better for beginners, but a board that is too big for your weight can be difficult to maneuver.

The advantages of a bigger board include being able to go out with less kite power and also kite in low winds, allowing you to stay afloat through mistakes made with the kite. When you start doing tricks and going upwind, a smaller board is more agile.

Boards also have different shapes for "cruising" versus doing jumps and tricks. Your personality will dictate what style appeals to you, so be sure to factor in your interests when you look into buying a board.

◊◊◊ Tips From Tyson ◊◊◊

A twin tip with a harder, stiffer, sharp, flat rail is going to work better for going upwind. Essentially it's going to be more efficient. But over time can be hard on the knees & back. Think of it more like a Porsche on stiff suspension.

A board with a rocker or deep channels makes for softer landings, and more of a cushiony type of ride. It's like a Cadillac with soft suspension, essentially making it less efficient.

It's best to learn and hone your skills on a little bit larger board. Not too big, though, and avoid learning on a light-wind specific board.

The Harness

The harness wraps around your hips or waist and has a metal hook on the front for the kite to attach to. The hook is on a "spreader bar" that spans the front of your hips. The harness is what connects you to the kite and directs the power of the kite to your body rather than making you just use only arm strength to hang on to and control your kite.

There are several styles of harnesses available including belt, seat, and snow styles. A seat harness is best to start with. This type has leg straps and a broad back that scoops down under your rear end so that the kite is not pulling on your back, but, instead, lifting on your body. There is a handle on the back that allows someone to hold you down if you are getting lifted off the ground when you don't want to be airborne.

Harnesses with legs, which are very much like rock climbing harnesses, are also available. A strap wraps around each leg, and there is a band right under the rear end. This type is especially good for snow kiting because, unlike water boarding where you are standing on your board all the time, you are sitting in your harness when you lift off the hill in snow.

There will be a hook or a cable to which you can attach a safety leash. In most kiting zones this leash is required, so be sure to use yours. There are a few experts who don't use one, but everyone who is starting out needs a leash because it keeps your kite from taking off when you lose control of it. Serious damage can be done by an out-of-control kite. The leash attaches to the bar and onto one of the lines that attach to the kite.

◊◊◊ Tips From Tyson ◊◊◊

Find the right size harness for you. Try several on and see how they contort and work with your body type and personal preference. You don't want the harness to move or twist. When I use a waist harness, I have mine so tight that I can't take in a full breath.

Also, don't go too small. The smaller the harness, the less surface area you have for distribution of force, and you increase the risk for injury.

The Control Bar

The control bar, often just shortened to "bar," is your steering mechanism and connects you to the kite via your lines. The lines that control the kite connect directly to the center and ends of the bar, and the bar connects to the front of your harness by a loop called the "chicken loop," which transfers your weight to the harness so that you aren't left hanging from the kite by just your arm strength. There is also a leash that connects from the side of your harness to the bar. This prevents your kite from flying away in the event that you release the chicken loop to depower the kite, prevents loss or damages to your equipment, and more importantly, prevents injury to bystanders.

Every manufacturer has its own designs, and each design will have differences from other styles offered by the same company. For this reason it is very important that you get proper instruction in the set up and operation of the exact make and model of the equipment that you will be using.

The design of the lines and bar set up involves incredible feats of aerodynamics, but you don't need to understand the theory behind the design to get started. Just be sure to carefully follow the manufacturer's instructions for a beginner set up, which will give you the most forgiving handling and easiest escape from troubling situations.

You can progress to a stock set up once you develop some skill and don't need to frequently release the kite, but again, be certain to follow manufacturer's guidance for your particular equipment and use a safe, standard set up. There are a lot of different places to hook in your safety leash, and experts who are doing high-powered jumps and stunts don't want the kite to depower immediately when they release the bar, so they set up their release mechanisms accordingly. As a beginner, you *do* want the kite to depower as soon as you release it, so the control bar is set for that extra level of safety.

The sections of Chapter 4 which describe the "suicide connection," "double

2: Getting Started with Kiting | **25**

depower," or "one release" set ups are for advanced riders; you won't need any of them until you have an advanced level of riding experience.

◊◊◊ Tips From Tyson ◊◊◊

Reducing the length of your lines drastically decreases the potential power your kite can generate. If you are still putting things together and have to fly in strong winds (20+ knots), a short-line setup (i.e. 20 meters down to 14 meters) is a great way to ease into those conditions with your smaller kites in the 4-8m range.

Pre-stretch lines so that your kite will fly straight for longer and not need tuning so soon.

◊◊◊

HowToKiteSurf.com

Chapter 2 FAQs & Common Misconceptions

Q: I've been surfing for 10 years, and I've parachuted out of planes. I can skip the lesson, right?

A: It's not the answer you were hoping to hear, but NO. Even experts in other sports should take a lesson before kiting. Remember, even experts in *this* sport have died in accidents from freak winds. The purpose of the lesson is to cover the basics, ensure that you understand the factors unique to this sport, and know what to do in an unexpected situation.

◇◇◇ Tips From Tyson ◇◇◇

> There is no replacement for lessons. Your life, or even avoiding a visit to the ER, is worth more than the cost of lessons. Also if you can't afford lessons, you can't afford proper equipment, so should consider another sport.

◇◇◇

Q: Paying for a trainer just seems like an added expense. Isn't it just a way for dealers to make more money?

A: Not at all. If you consider the costs of even a minor accident, the price of a trainer is a small expense. Logging time with a trainer builds your skills and confidence so that you are more able to enjoy a full-size kite, and remember – a few dealers will even apply the amount spent on a trainer kite to a full-size kite when you buy one from them. It certainly can't hurt to ask and everybody wins.

◇◇◇ Tips From Tyson ◇◇◇

> If you can fly the trainer at your local spot, it will help you learn things you normally wouldn't have any way of knowing, like wind shadows, where the wind might swirl or get lofty, etc. Make sure to do your best to keep it dry—a wet trainer kite won't fly very well.

◇◇◇

Chapter 3:
Safety

How to Safely Operate Your Equipment

Kiteboarding is the fastest growing sport in the world and is expected to keep growing in popularity. The International Sailing Federation (ISAF) has even looked at replacing windsurfing with kiteboarding in the Olympics. In 2012, the ISAF council decided to make the switch for the 2016 Games in Rio, but the ISAF General Assembly later overturned the vote, reinstating windsurfing. There is still the potential for kiteboarding to be included in the 2020 Summer Olympics, so excitement will be building as nations all over the world start developing competitive teams.

With more and more people getting active in the sport and looking for new places to participate, it becomes even more important than ever for all of us to know how to kite safely. This chapter contains information that you want to learn well and refer back to often. It's going to cover where you can kite, when it's safe to go out, and how to interact peaceably with others.

The next chapter is going to cover how to safely operate your equipment, so it's another valuable reference to keep nearby while you are in the learning process. Don't be intimidated by all the new terms; that's why you have this guide. You can look up anything you aren't too sure about any time you need to.

The Kiting Environment: What Makes for a Safe Place to Kite?

When a serious kiting injury occurs, it's usually when a kiter smashes in to a solid object: a wall, a vehicle, a tree.... You get the picture. You need to make sure that nothing is downwind of you.

You want flat snow, sand, or water. When you are starting out with a larger kite, you want to have at least 2-3 football fields (200-300 yards) of clear space downwind of you. If you are starting out at the beach, you want wide, sandy beach and shallow water with a sandy bottom. Make sure there are no obstacles, including the less obvious ones like rocks in shallow water or volleyball nets.

Be sure you check in with the locals wherever you go. Most people in the kiting community like to help out and are great sources of information about local regulations, which areas are best and worst for kiting, hidden dangers in the water, and local weather patterns. That said, remember that no matter how good the advice you get from the locals, *you* must understand the wind to kite safely!

Between kiteboarding, kite surfing, snow kiting, and land boarding, you can find a place to enjoy kiting just about anywhere there's wind. In this sport, though, the wind is the proverbial "blessing and a curse." It is a natural force that you cannot control, and while you can't kite without it, it is also the major hazard you will encounter. Injuries can result from colliding with any solid object – including the ground – and when that happens it's usually because of an unexpected wind event during a time of high or gusty winds.

Safety Rule #1: Know Your Wind...
And Only Go Out When You Know It Is Safe

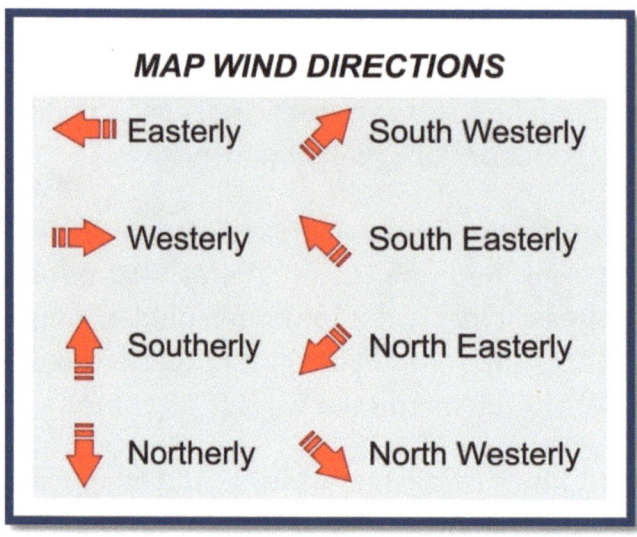

The Internet is your best source of wind information. You can get general information quickly from the local weather station on TV, but online sources will give you much more complete information. You may even have access to live webcam footage of your site.

You can use this information to make decisions about where to go and what kind of gear to take with you, but the bottom line is going to reflect what the wind is doing when you arrive. Regardless of what was reported, you have to assess the conditions on the spot. Pay attention to how the sky looks, how other kites are flying, wind socks, and any other indicators that you have available.

Listen to the wind. You can tell a lot about how steady it is by the sound. Is it constant or intermittent? Gusty conditions are much more difficult and should be avoided.

◇◇◇ Tips From Tyson ◇◇◇

Stormy conditions or dark clouds are definitely conditions suited only for the experts or for people with very little worth living for.

◇◇◇

Another great indicator is the locals. If they are all sitting on the shore watching one maniac on a kite, it's a good sign that you should join the majority on this one. "Wind dummy" and "guinea pig" are terms used by kiteboarders to refer to the one person who goes out to test the wind.

Even after you have gotten a little kiteboarding under your belt, it is still a good idea to go back to your trainer kite. The trainer lets you get a feel for what the winds do to a kite, and you can practice handling it in inconsistent circumstances. Caution is still required, particularly if you are a lighter-weight person, because even a trainer kite can generate quite a bit of power under the right conditions, and injuries have occurred when the winds were too strong.

If you have been beached for a while and the winds seem good for kiting again, remember that your launching angle will depend on actual conditions at that very moment, regardless of what's been going on through the rest of the day. If the wind has increased in speed or direction, be sure to take a fresh look at what is now downwind and evaluate that direction for any hazards.

Best Winds for Kiteboarding

You want steady, clean wind, and in order to get that you need to be 50-100 yards downwind of a building or big tree. Why? Because the smooth flow of the wind becomes turbulent when it is broken up by a large object. It takes up to 100 yards for it to settle back into a smooth pattern.

Gusts

Sudden, hard winds are called poltergusts, and they can wreak havoc on a kite. When the wind is coming in short bursts instead of a sustained flow, you have gusty conditions. If you are out on the water and see a bunch of spray coming toward you, it's caused by a gust and you need to get your kite down and avoid it if possible. On snow, a gust will look like a big swirl of snow, and here, too, you'll want to keep your kite out of it.

Never get your lines wrapped around your fingers (or any body part) because if your kite catches a strong gust, it will put a tremendous amount of pull on the lines, and they have been known to cut right through flesh in that situation.

Wind Direction

When referring to the compass direction of wind, we say the direction from which it is coming. (e.g. a northerly wind is coming from the north, so your downwind would be to the south.)

The directions used this way include northerly, southerly, easterly, westerly, north easterly, north westerly, south easterly, and south westerly. These directions will be shown on a wind map, which you should check before you go out each time.

The significance of each of these will depend on your geographic location. On the beach in Tampa, Florida, a westerly will likely be a sea breeze off the Gulf, whereas if you are on the Great Lakes in the northern U.S., depending on which shore you are on, a westerly could be coming off a hill towards the water or across the lake towards the shore.

For kiteboarding purposes, the main direction we are concerned with isn't north-south-east-west, but, instead, which way the wind is blowing in relation to the beach. This is also called the wind condition.

◊◊◊ Tips From Tyson ◊◊◊

Turning your palms into the wind can help you indicate the true direction of the wind.

Onshore: *The wind blows toward shore from the sea.* This can be good for kitesurfing but is difficult for beginners because it tends to put you right back on the beach. Do not go out in strong onshore winds because they will tend to blow you inland and risks injuring you or someone else.

Offshore: *The wind blows from the land out to sea.* You don't want to be out in an offshore wind unless you are an expert, AND you have a backup boat to rescue you if you get blown out. As a beginning to intermediate level kiteboarder, do not go out in offshore winds. The chances of getting taken out to sea are just too great.

Side On: *The wind blows toward the beach at an angle to the water's edge.* This is ideal for beginners because it's safe but gives you a chance to do something before you are deposited on the sand.

Side Off: *The wind blows from the beach at a sideways angle rather than going directly out to sea.* Depending on the angle this may not be too bad, but beware of any wind that will take you out to sea.

Cross Wind: *The wind blows parallel the shoreline.* Ideal for beginner kiteboarders, but unfortunately it's not that common for the wind to follow the water's edge. If you are on a big body of water, the wind is usually coming off the water toward land.

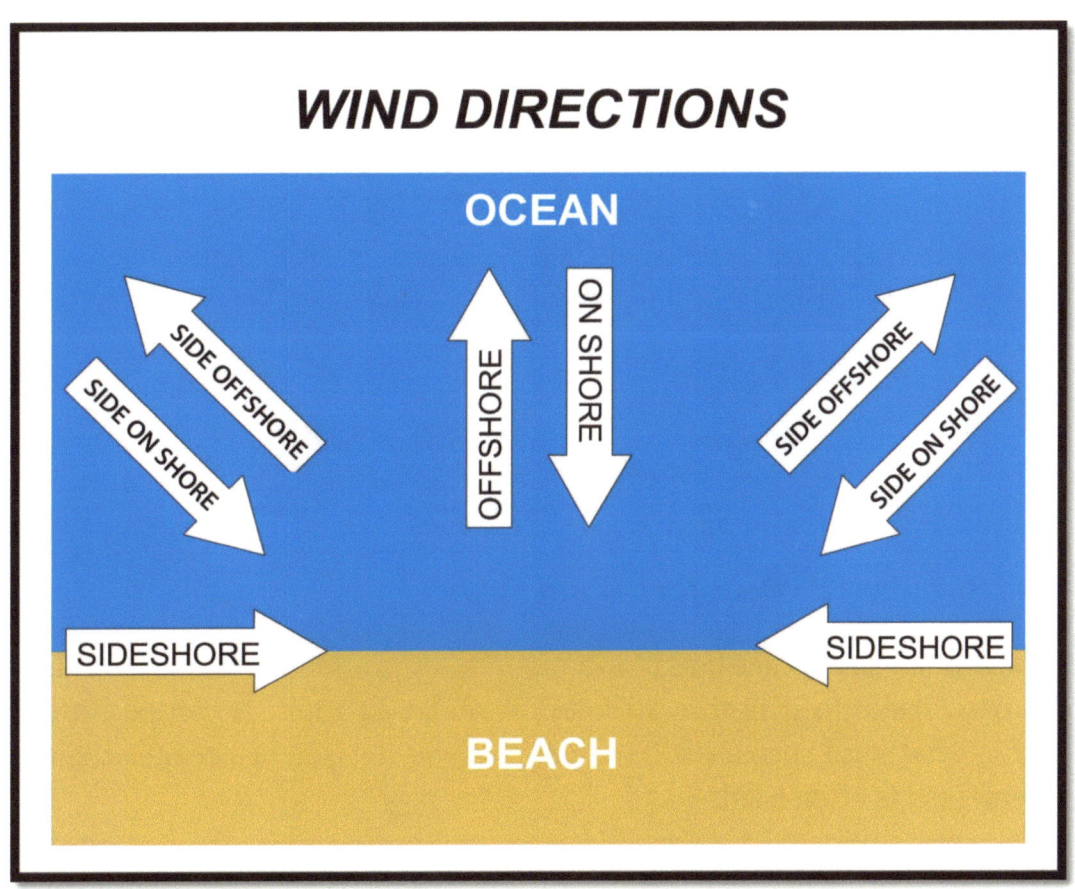

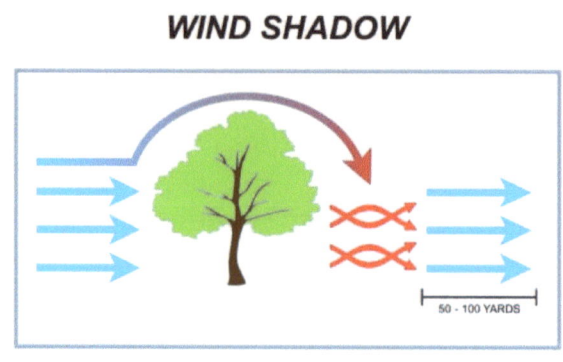

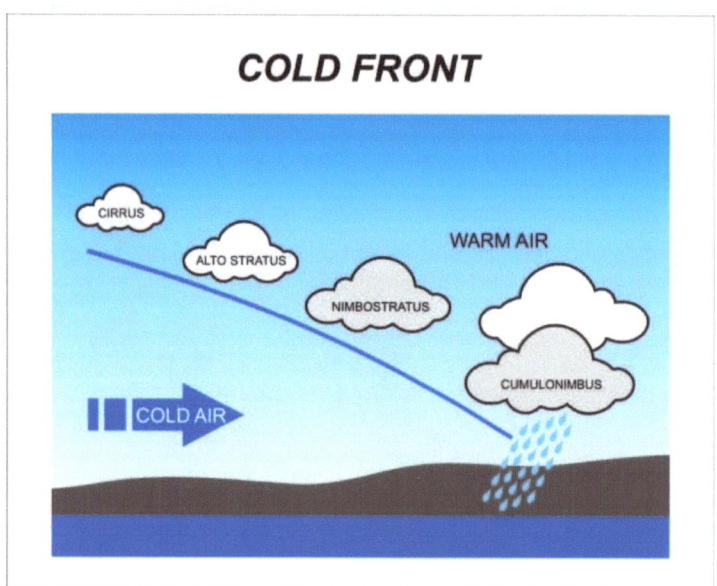

Safe Wind Speeds: The Beaufort Wind Scale

Wind speed is usually measured in knots. A knot is about 1.15 miles per hour, so an easy way to relate to it is that 10 knots is about 12 mph. It can be difficult to conceptualize what wind speeds do, so a scale that was devised before measuring tools were implemented is often used.

Originally conveying the strength of the wind by stating the number of sails that a ship would be using, the current Beaufort Wind Scale uses numbers to represent ranges of effects. For example, the scale starts at zero, which indicates complete calm in which smoke from a chimney would rise vertically. A 32-38 on the scale is a moderate gale, which means whole trees are in motion, and you would experience inconvenience in walking against the wind. A 73 or higher on the scale indicate winds in the hurricane ranges.

BEAUFORT NUMBER	WIND	SYMBOL	WIND SPEED (MPH)
0	CALM	○	LESS THAN 1
1	LIGHT AIR	○—	1-3
2	SLIGHT BREEZE	○—	4-7
3	GENTLE BREEZE	○—|	8-12
4	MODERATE BREEZE	○—||	13-18
5	FRESH BREEZE	○—|||	19-24
6	STRONG BREEZE	○—|||	25-31
7	MODERATE GALE	○—||||	32-38
8	FRESH GALE	○—||||	39-46
9	STRONG GALE	○—|||||	47-54
10	WHOLE GALE	○—||||	55-63
11	STORM	○—|||||	64-75
12	HURRICANE	○—|||||	MORE THAN 75

As you can see, the Beaufort scale is very sensory-oriented and allows you to quickly determine an environmental condition by being given the number. You can use the scale to estimate wind speeds based on your observations of the effects of the wind.

For example, when the trees are not swaying but there is enough wind that small branches are moving and dust and leaves are getting picked up, then you know you have a moderate breeze at 19-24 mph. Familiarize yourself with the scale, and learn the indicators that tell you when the wind is at a safe speed for kiteboarding.

Wind Speed for Trainer Kites

When you are starting with a trainer kite, you want to go out when the winds are approximately 8 to 15 knots. This wind range assures enough wind to use your trainer kite, but not so much that you can't get good practice on your form.

CONVERSION TABLE FOR KNOTS TO MILES PER HOUR

KTS TO MPH	
5 Knots = 5.8 MPH	80 Knots = 92.2 MPH
10 Knots = 11.5 MPH	85 Knots = 97.9 MPH
15 Knots = 17.3 MPH	90 Knots = 103.7 MPH
20 Knots = 23.0 MPH	95 Knots = 109.4 MPH
25 Knots = 28.8 MPH	100 Knots = 115.2 MPH
30 Knots = 34.6 MPH	105 Knots = 121.0 MPH
35 Knots = 40.3 MPH	110 Knots = 126.7 MPH
40 Knots = 46.1 MPH	115 Knots = 132.5 MPH
45 Knots = 51.8 MPH	120 Knots = 138.2 MPH
50 Knots = 57.6 MPH	125 Knots = 144.0 MPH
55 Knots = 63.4 MPH	130 Knots = 149.8 MPH
60 Knots = 69.1 MPH	135 Knots = 155.5 MPH
65 Knots = 74.9 MPH	140 Knots = 161.3 MPH
70 Knots = 80.6 MPH	145 Knots = 167.0 MPH
75 Knots = 86.4 MPH	150 Knots = 172.8 MPH

You want to work with the trainer kite until you can maneuver it the way you want to without looking at it. You need gentle, steady winds to get a feel for the kite and its handling. Before you consider yourself fully trained you will want to get some experience with somewhat rougher conditions, but to get started, work in normal wind conditions so you can focus on your technique.

After you get a feel for the kite and learn how to maneuver it, get out in some higher winds. The trainer kite is the perfect tool for practicing dealing with stronger winds and less-than-ideal conditions.

Safe Wind Speed for Kiteboarding

When you are starting to get up on a board with a full-sized kite, be certain to only go out when the wind is in the range of 10-14 knots. Practice on a day with steady winds.

You may be able to practice body dragging if the wind is under 10 knots, but it will be difficult to get enough power to get up on the board.

The Weather

There are a few terms you should know as we go into a discussion on the weather. "Downwind" is key term and refers to the direction the wind is going. For training purposes, you are always facing downwind.

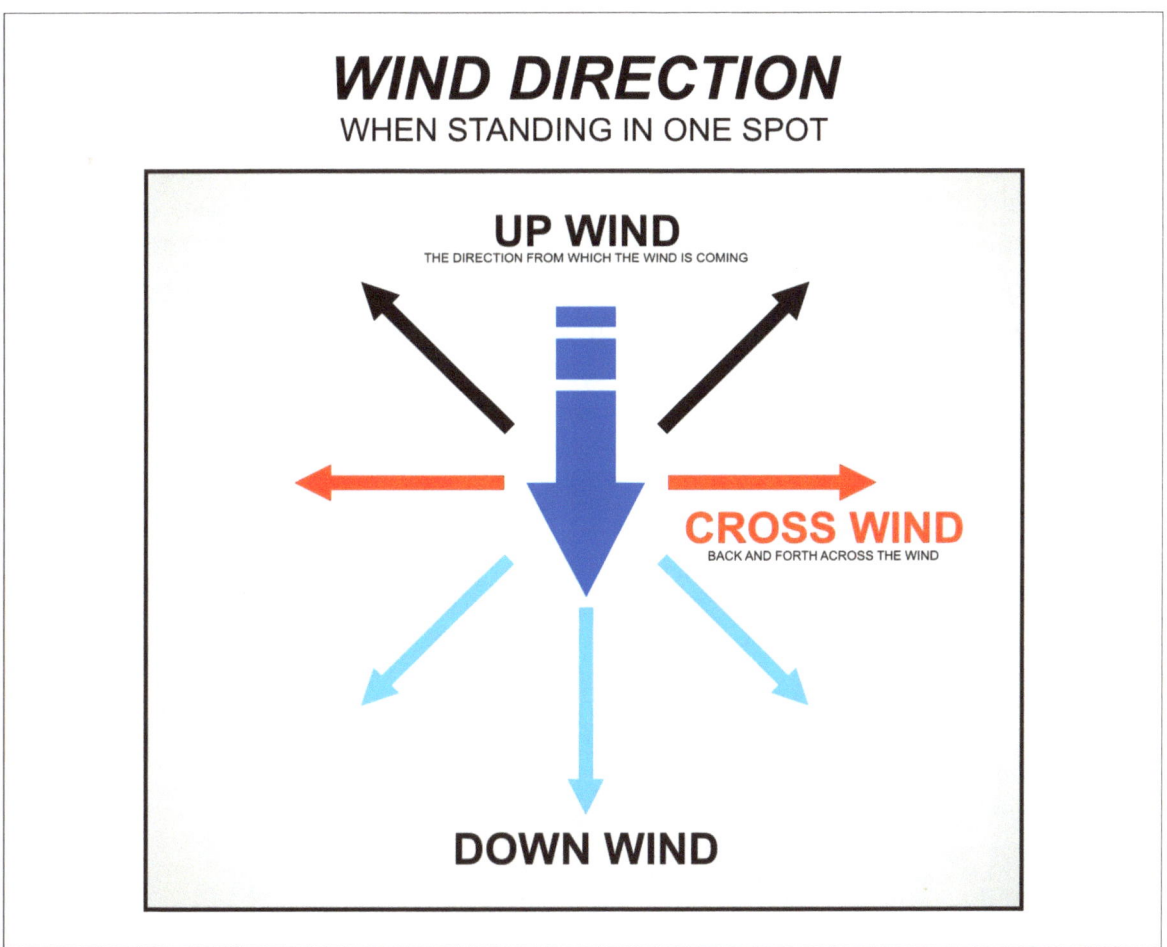

Think of it this way: The wind is all around you, but the only area you have to be concerned with is the area in which your kite can fly. It can't fly behind you – only downwind of you – and it can't fly further away than the length of your lines. The area you are concerned about is limited to the "wind window."

The Wind Window

"Wind window" is a key kitesurfing term that refers to the area your kite moves around in. It includes the half-dome shaped area created by the full extension of your kite's reach from the arc created by extension out from your left side, over your head and out to your right side, and as far forward, right, and left as your kite can reach (see illustration). These are determined by the length of your lines (typically 21 meters, or 69 feet).

One way we talk about the wind window is to think of it as a clock face. Directly above you is the zenith at 12:00. Nine o'clock is straight out to your left and 3:00 is to your right. Use the illustration to get familiar with this scheme because you will be hearing a lot about 11:00, 1:00, and other references to the clock locations.

Keep in mind that your wind window moves with you. You have to pay attention to the entire distance in front of you and out to both sides. When you start practicing your moves you'll be walking around, and it's easy to lose track of how far you have moved, so keep an eye on your horizon for the whole area inside the wind window.

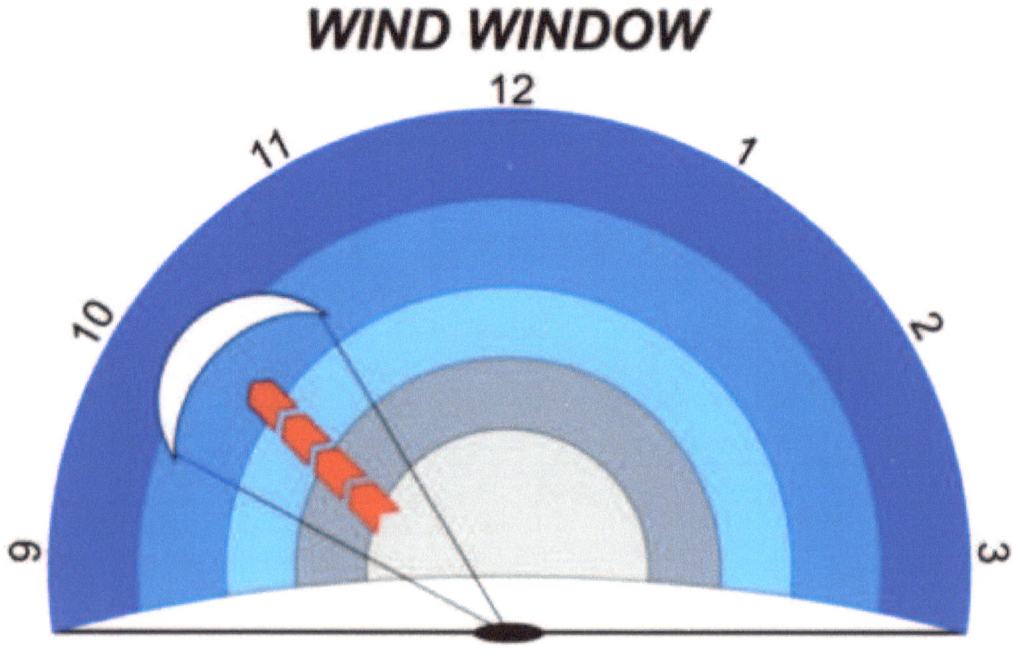

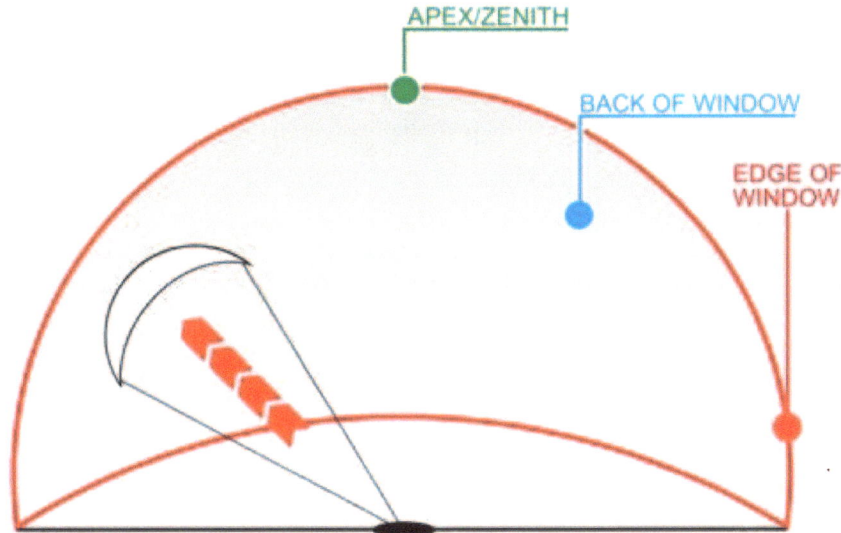

Your kite can go forward (downwind) and out to either side at any angle. When you are starting to learn how to handle a kite, be sure you have someone with you who can make sure other people, dogs, etc. stay out of the entire area of your wind window. Remember, the wind can change directions suddenly, but it can also just stop and send your kite plummeting to the ground. This is often called the "Hindenberg" effect. A falling kite can hurt someone, so be sure your whole area stays clear.

Get out with your trainer kite and get a feel for how big the area is and how freely your kite can move around in it.

Neutral Zones

Your neutral zone is the leading edge of your wind window, which arcs from just overhead and extends out to both sides of you. That's where you can most safely park the kite while it's flying. Practice getting your kite into the neutral zone.

Zenith

The area directly overhead is the highest point the kite can attain. Unfortunately, although it is very stable at the zenith, the kite becomes vulnerable to lofting (see lofting section in Chapter 5). That's why the neutral zones (out to the sides) is where you want to park your kite.

Power Zones

As the kite swings downwind of you into an angle from 30 to 70 degrees from the ground, it enters the "power zone." This is where it catches the most wind and generates the most force. The kite will have the greatest force when traveling directly downwind and between these two angles.

We refer to the surface area of the kite that is catching the wind as "seeing the wind." When the kite is directly in front of you, the full surface will capture wind, making the power zone the area where your kite will really pull. Move your kite through the power zone, but don't let it sit there too long or you will lose control of it.

Sharing Space: Who Has the Right of Way?

Kiters and surfers often have designated areas in which they can practice their sport. If you go to a new area and notice that all the kiters are in one area, it probably means that kiting is only allowed in that zone. It's important that you not kite in other, unauthorized areas because violations can end up getting everyone banned (and that's certainly no way to make friends in the kiting community)!

Swimmers always have the right of way, and you should always be downwind of them. As far as boats and surfers are concerned, whoever has the greater steering capability is obligated to yield the right of way. It may not sound fair, but it makes sense from a safety point of view.

The craft with less inherent controllability gets the right of way. For example, sailboats have the right of way with respect to motorboats but not with surfers. A wind surfer has more ability to steer than a board surfer, so the board surfer gets the right of way.

Kite surfers are considered to have more control than wind surfers, so we give them the right of way and stay downwind of them. Likewise, if you encounter a board surfer, steer clear and give them the right of way.

3: Safety | 41

Always look downwind before setting up to jump.

Advanced kiters give beginners the right of way by staying away from them, but as a beginner you must pay close attention to where you are going so you don't crowd someone out and cause a collision.

Right of Way with Other Kiters

So we've defined the kiting zone, but how do we keep from running over each other?

Launching

The kite that is launching has the right of way, so you may have to take another tack if you are landing.

Always consider others when kiting and know your right of way. Use situational awareness at all times.

Passing in Opposite Directions

Say, for example, that you are kiting away from the shore in a side on wind, and you come towards someone heading for the beach. What do you do?

You should first acknowledge one another. Then, the person in the upwind position should put his kite in a high position in the neutral zone. The downwind person should lower her kite in the wind window.

Kite set up is consistent and when two people are moving in opposite directions, one will have his right hand forward and the other will have the left. The upwind person with his right hand forward will have right of way.

Know your right of way when kiting close to other kiters.

Kite surfers generally feel like a community and like to help each other, so if you get confused or forget how things work, don't hesitate to ask somebody. For your safety as well as those around you, you must practice kite control and learn the standard etiquette of the sport. While most people think of etiquette in terms of mere niceties, in this kind of sport, etiquette is about safety. Keep in mind that if you violate the rules that keep us all safe, someone is going to set you straight – and it's much easier to ask beforehand than to get told off about it afterwards!

Know where to place your kite in the wind window when passing another rider.

Communication: Vocabulary and Hand Signals

Kiting, like many sports, involves working with others when you can't communicate verbally. Whether kiters are too far apart or it's just particularly difficult to hear over the wind, hand signals are an important part of communicating while kiting. For safety's sake, it's important to learn the standard meanings so that you know what's going on around you and others can understand what you're trying to communicate. Below are some essential phrases and corresponding signals that every kiteboarder should know by heart.

Launch the Kite

Give a thumbs-up with your arm extended to one side to signal everything is "OKAY" to launch the kite.

Go Toward the Water

Motion toward the water with fingers and arms pointing up – then in the direction to go. This may also be used to motion to a kiter to move away from a populated beach area.

Come In to Shore
Motion same as above, pointing in the direction to go.

48 | How to Kitesurf

"HELP"
Wave your arms above your head.

Land the Kite

Gently pat your head to signal for someone to assist in catching and landing your kite. Wait for the same signal for a confirmation from the assistant.

Watch Me
Point your fingers to your eyes.

Put Down Your Kite
Place both arms out to the side, bend at the elbows, and point down.

Put Your Kite at 12 o'clock
Point to the sky or make a point with your arms and fingers.

Problems with Your Gear
Wave your bar above your head.

Safety Equipment

Many safety features are built into your harness, control bar, and kite, but all of them must be used according to manufacturer's instructions if you expect to stay safe. However, listed below are a few additional pieces of gear that you should strongly consider using for further safety measures.

Helmet — A helmet is recommended when kiteboarding to provide some protection against cuts and blunt trauma to the head. A rogue gust can toss you against something solid, but accidents may happen even under normal kiting circumstances. You can get hit by your board or bar, fall against rocks that you didn't know were under the water, or have an encounter with a rogue (read "rude") boater. While accidents are unlikely if you're following all of the proper procedures, you never know what will happen, and helmets will keep your precious skull safe in the event of an accident.

Whistle — A whistle is a simple and potentially lifesaving safety tool in this sport, and you can often find kiteboarding knives with whistles built into the casing. It can be difficult for others to find you in the water, so it's a good idea to have a whistle on you so that you can easily make noise should you end up needing assistance. It can also be used to call attention to yourself if you are giving a hand signal that isn't being seen.

Safety Hook Knife — This special corrosion-resistant knife with a blade protected by a curved plastic hook – a safety hook knife – should be included with your gear. Some harnesses have a special pocket for this small knife, but the knife is designed with a metal loop on the end for attachment to the harness if there is not pocket available. The knife can be used should you become entangled in your lines or if lines get snagged on something.

Flotation Device — A personal flotation device (PFD) is recommended if you are out in deep water and may actually be required if you are using any kind of water craft for backup. PFDs are an inexpensive safety choice for a number of fairly obvious reasons, but if you insist on heading out on the water without one, check out the local laws first to ensure that you stay in compliance.

Leash — If you have to release your kite, a kite leash will prevent it from flying away downwind and getting in the way of boaters (or worse, possibly injuring someone). The leash connects to the kite by only one line, so a kite on a leash will just flap in the wind rather than flying with any power. As an additional safety feature, kite leashes have a release mechanism at the attachment point in case your kite becomes wrapped around something or is otherwise dragging you into danger.

To detach the leash, manually grab the release mechanism where it attaches to your harness and pull it away from your body; the kite will pop loose. A leash that keeps your kite from blowing away when you use your release is standard, but *board* leashes are not used in kiteboarding. They have been found to cause board injuries, so be prepared to swim after your board if you take a fall.

Kitemares

"Kitemare" is a common term for kiteboarding incidents that prove to be horrifying. Of course, people use the term loosely. An incident may be as small as staying out too long and having to hike half a mile up the beach in the dark, as awful as finding yourself being pulled out to sea and having to ditch your well-loved and expensive equipment so you can swim back to shore, or as terrifying as being lofted and thrown into a large and very solid object.

Anyone that spends much time at the sport will have a kitemare eventually (kind of like motorcyclists and "road rash"), but there is a "lesson learned" in almost every case. If it takes having a kitemare incident to remind you of a safety precept that you've neglected to follow (thus preventing future injury), the lesson learned may well be worth it. After a kitemare, you'll never again say things like, "I'm too excited to read all the instructions," or "the winds are a little strong, but I can handle it by myself." Maybe you can; maybe you can't. Either way, err on the side of caution.

I suggested early on that you go online and look at videos of kiteboarding accidents. You'll find some videos of beginners getting banged up, intermediates telling stories of how they blew it and broke a leg, and even newscasts reporting on experts getting lofted and smashed into the ground. The more you understand about what can happen, the better you can prepare to keep yourself safe – and I bet your family would appreciate your caution as well!

Accidents do happen but just as in everything else in life, kiting forces you to make quick decisions that will determine whether you walk out of a situation safely. Don't let your ego get the better of you and cause you to take on too much or take risks beyond your skill level. One of the great perks about kiting is that even the practice is fun, so work on each of your skills until they are really solid.

If your training indicates that conditions aren't right for you, don't let anyone pressure you into going out. It's far better to feel a little frustrated (while sitting on a beautiful beach, no less) than it is to get a patient's-eye-view of the back of an ambulance.

It's important to rest when necessary, even if you are out on the water.

Chapter 3 FAQs & Common Misconceptions

Q: I've seen those kitemare videos online. If even experts can get killed, can I really do this safely?

A: Kiteboarding is considered an extreme sport, and there is a certain amount of risk involved. However, bear in mind that you have a lot of control over how much risk you take. Many experts who have been injured in kiting accidents will tell you that it happened because they either went out when they knew the weather was bad or because they got careless and did something that they knew they shouldn't do. You can be very conservative in determining the weather, wind conditions, and the locations that are acceptable for you.

International Right of Way Rules

Never kite alone.

Before going out, check wind conditions and the weather forecast.

In addition to the sailing rules, find out the local rules and boundaries of the kitesurfing area.

Respect the boundaries of the designated kitesurfing area.

Your kite leash, quick release and depowering safety device are not optional. Use them for the safety of those around you as well as yourself.

Avoid crowded areas for launching and landing.

Never pass over non-kiteboarders when launching or jumping.

Limit the length of any ride to the distance you can swim.

Keep a safe distance from power lines and any other obstructions (look all around!)

Outgoing kiter has the right of way—yield if you are incoming.

Launching kiter has the right of way—yield if you are landing.

Distance yourself from windsurfers so they are never in your kite's power zone.

Yield right of way to all non-powered water users.

Chapter 4: Equipment Operation

Before You Launch – Tools That Could Save Your Time and Life

Now that you know the "what" and "where" of kiting, let's talk about the "how." Before we get into the technical details of handling your equipment, I'd like to give you a tool that will save you a lot of time and effort.

Visualization

It has been proven time and again that visualization enhances sport performance, and it's very simple to do. You just think about what it is that you want to do, close your eyes, and see it happening in your mind's eye. If you can imagine the feelings, smells, etc. that accompany the action, the results will be even better.

Before you get your kite in the air to practice figure 8s, close your eyes and imagine yourself holding the bar; picture the kite rising. You can extend your physical arm if you like and pantomime the actions, but if pantomiming the visualized action would make you feel too self-conscious, you certainly don't have to. Either way, try to feel the connection through your body as you visualize handling your bar and controlling your kite.

Setting Up & Practicing with a Trainer Kite

Once you've found an appropriate place to practice, don't be shy about getting out with your trainer kite. You will make some mistakes and maybe even manage some

4: Equipment Operation | 59

spectacular crashes, but that's what the trainer kite is for. You don't want to tear it up being foolish, but get the most out of it by learning basic maneuvers before pushing your limits a little. You should get in at *least* ten hours of practice with the trainer before you attach yourself to a full-sized kite.

Get out on a gusty day to get a feel for managing unpredictable situations. Let your body get a sense for how to compensate for various levels of force on the kite. Everything you learn with your trainer kite translates directly into better skills on your full sized kite. After you start kiting, it's a good idea to hang on to your trainer kite so you can use it for practice when you are ready to try out higher winds or tricky moves.

Watch for loose dogs or children running on the beach when setting up, launching, and landing your kite

Check the pressure in the leading edge and the struts.

The basic design of your equipment will be consistent from one manufacturer to another. There is a system of color coding that is used by all of them to make the sport safer and easier to learn. For example, the control bar will have red or orange on the left side and usually green, blue, or gray on the right. Some have three color bands – a narrower yellow band marks the center, the left side is marked in red, and the right side is marked in blue. This way you will always be able to match up the corresponding left and right sides of your kite and the bar.

The design of your trainer kite is simple. The long edges are called the "leading edge" and "trailing edge," while the ends are referred to as "wing tips." Full-sized kites generally use the same naming system for parts but may refer to the leading edge as the "forward edge" or "top edge," while the trailing edge is called the "back end."

The line attachments on both the kite and bar are called "pigtails." The line attachments on a kite should have a loop in the end that is used to attach the kite to the lines from the bar. Your bar lines will have a reinforced piece at the end, and the lines will usually be knotted together.

4: Equipment Operation | 61

Hold the kite upside down facing the wind when carrying the kite.

When you unpack your trainer kite, put a weight or some sand on the bag to keep it from blowing away. Then, as you lay out your kite, put sand on the trailing edge so it doesn't launch before you are ready.

To attach the lines you will use a lark's head knot. To do this, feed the line from the kite through the loop at the end, creating a new adjustable loop (see illustration). This is the same kind of loop that is used on the end of yo-yo strings to make an adjustable loop or to secure a helium balloon to a toddler's arm. Then you simply feed the bar line through the loop and tighten it around the line so the knot is held in place.

Walk away from the kite, laying down the lines as you go. They must be straight enough to remain untangled, but keep some slack or you will accidentally launch the kite before you are ready. When you are at the end of the lines, you may need to twist the bar around to unwind them if they have become twisted up. You should be able to look down the lines and see that each one goes straight to the kite with no tangles.

If there is any concern about your lines becoming tangled with the prior method, there is another way to set up which some people actually prefer. Begin by laying out your kite with the trailing edge weighted; then take your lines and walk out until you've just about reached their maximum length. Lay your bar on the ground with the blue end to the right; then take the blue lines in your right hand and the red lines in your left, and let the line lay down as you walk towards your kite. This assures the lines are laid out cleanly all the way to the kite before you even connect them.

Walk your lines out, checking for any crossed lines.

◊◊◊ Tips From Tyson ◊◊◊

If you run your lines and connect them to the kite with the bar upwind of the kite, then make sure to either tuck the rear/back/steering lines under the leading edge or at least have some have some slack in them. This way, when you flip over the kite to launch it, you won't have the line going over the top of the kite and making you have to rig all over again.

◊◊◊

Launching the Trainer Kite

Pick up the bar and hold it out horizontally in front of you with your right hand in the middle of the blue section and your left hand centered in the red. You don't want to hold the ends of the bar, so practice keeping your hands in this position.

Assisted Launch: For your first launches, try an assisted launch. When you are prepared to launch and have your bar ready, have someone else lift the leading edge. Let the kite come out of the sand as the wind fills the sails; this assures that the kite is in a good position when your assistant releases it. As you hold the bar steady, the kite will rise. Some kites launch better by lifting on one wing tip and letting the other end be free. Check your manufacturer's recommendations for your particular kite.

Solo Launch: From the ready position, you can slowly back away and as the lines become taut, the sails will fill with wind and the kite will lift off the ground.

Re-launching: Trainer kites are designed to launch easily. When your kite falls, take a step forward and let the kite lay over. The wind will get underneath the kite and cause it to lift back up. Don't try to make it fly by pulling on it like a regular kid's kite. That will just drag it through the sand.

Always wind your kite lines up in a figure 8 on the bar.

Landing: It's best to have a buddy ready to grab the kite when it lands. Have him stand just outside the wind window, and when the kite lands he should put some sand on it so it doesn't re-launch. You can also land it yourself by letting it lay down, then laying down your bar and walking to the kite while holding one line. When you get to the kite, be sure to put some sand on it so it can't get picked up by the wind.

Packing Up: Wrap your lines around the bar by bringing all the lines to the center, and wrap them around it a few times. Walk toward the kite, pulling all of the lines out evenly and wrapping them snugly around the ends of the bar in a figure 8 pattern.

When you reach the kite, fold it a few times and place it back on the sand, positioning the bar over the folded kite. The bar will give the kite some support as it is rolled around the bar. This helps keep things neat and makes it easier to fit everything back into the storage bag.

Controlling the Trainer Kite

Practice holding the bar at about waist height in front of you. You will want to avoid letting your arms reach above head level, and don't use sweeping arm swings to control the kite. It takes a lot of muscle to pull the kite around that way. Rather, think of the bar as a steering mechanism.

Putting your two hands on a bar can make you want to steer as though you are steering a car. What you want to do, though, is push and pull. When the kite is low, the motion is much like a punch, with one hand straight forward at a time. When dealing with a kite that is high in the air, the motion is more like climbing a ladder, with one hand moving up or down at a time.

Flow with the kite and practice pulling the bar. Pull right to make the kite go to the right; pull left to make it go left. Simple, right? When you've got that down, move on to figure 8s. If the trainer kite pulls too much when you are starting out, it's alright to sit down until you feel stable enough to stand up and try it again.

Practice controlling your trainer kite one-handed all over the wind window. Mentally divide the window into two halves, right and left. Practice doing figure 8s in the right and in the left halves. Do both horizontal and upright 8s, but note that the curved boundary of the wind window will angle the upright 8s so that they aren't actually vertical.

Once you have a feel for handling the kite, practice moving through the maximum power zone directly downwind of you, crossing the centerline. This is where you get the power to lift your body out of the water or off of the snow and into a standing position on top of your board.

Work with the trainer until you can control it without looking so that when you move on to a full-sized kite you will be able to handle it while you get on the board. You should be able to control your kite with one hand so you can use the other to get your board set up.

◊◊◊ Tips From Tyson ◊◊◊

If you have limited space, weigh less than 100 lbs, or are taking the trainer out in 17+ knots, I suggest shortening the lines by 50% of the standard length.

To do this, you first detach the lines from the kite.

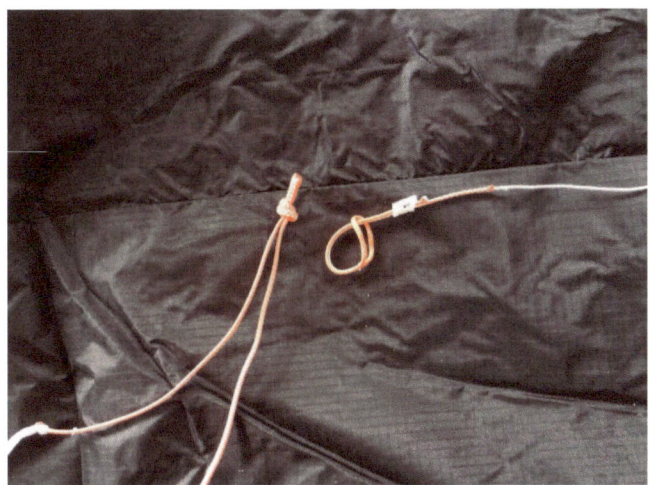

Run these connections back towards the bar and attach them to the leader line that comes off the bar. Make sure to attach them at the same point on the leader line on both sides so that the line length will be equal.

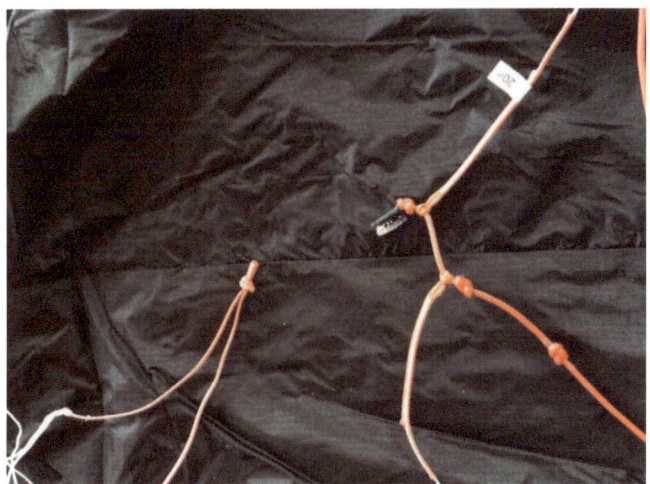

Now find the new end point for your lines.

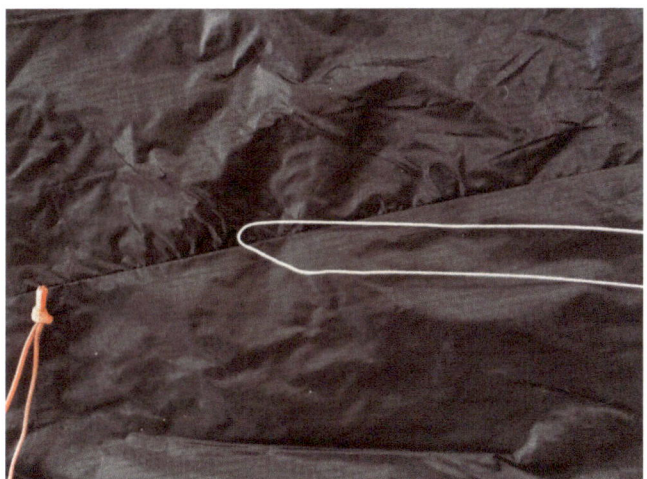

Make a loop—to do this make an A-ok sign with your fingers, put them through the loop, open them and reconnect to make the A-ok sign again, but on the back side of the line.

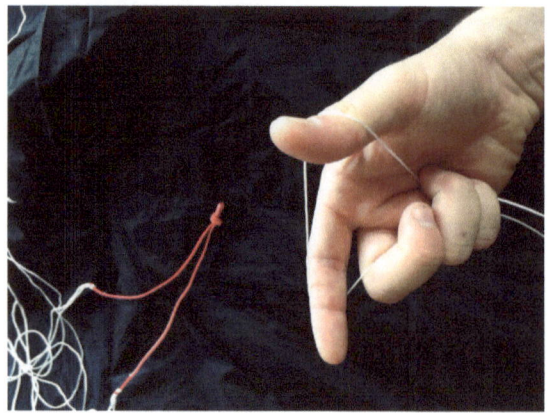

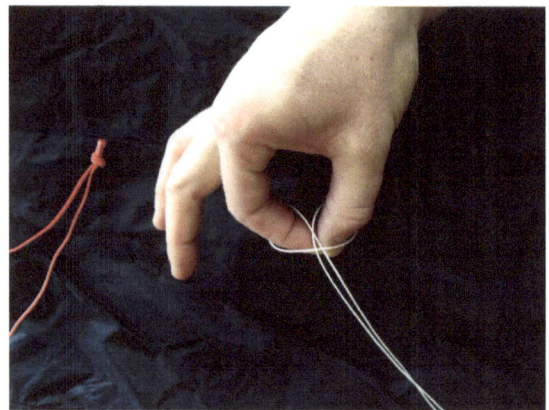

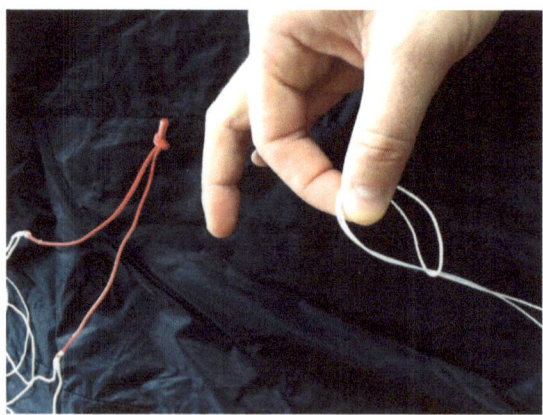

4: Equipment Operation | **67**

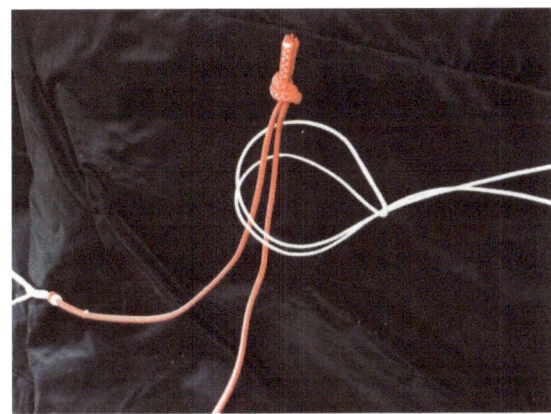

You now have a lark's head loop, and can again attach the line to the kite. Do this with both sides and you will have lines that are stronger, more durable and half the length.

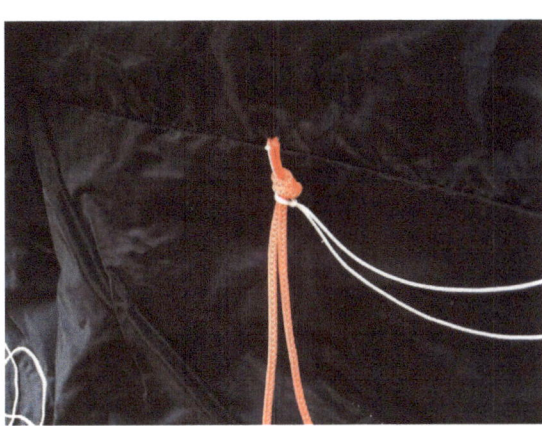

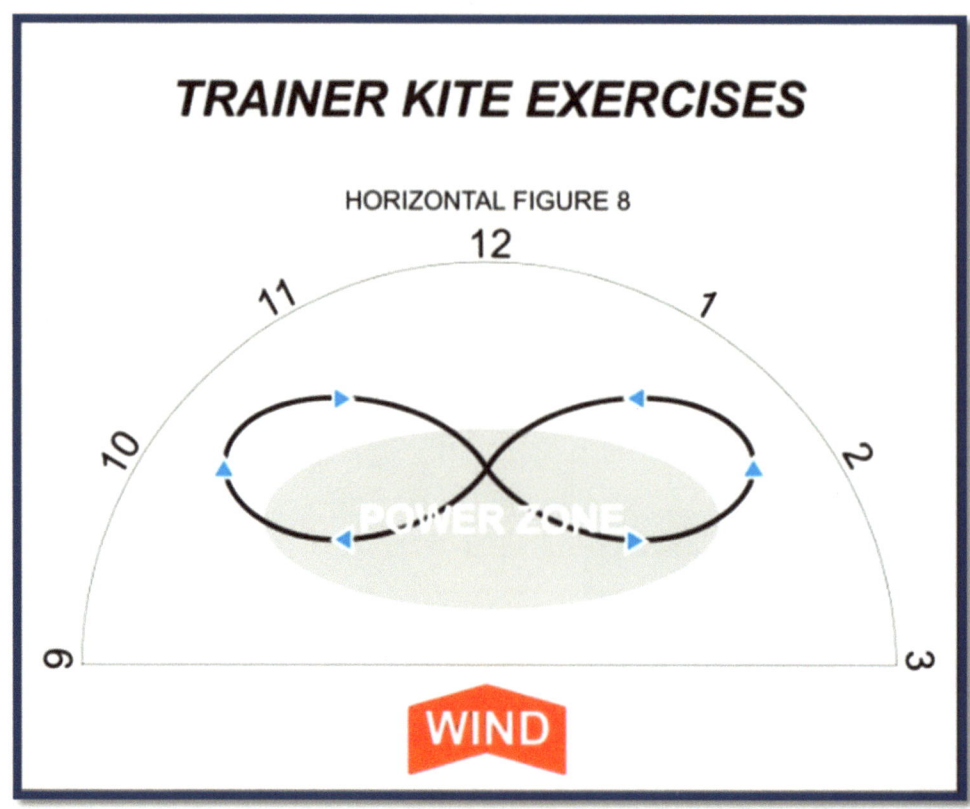

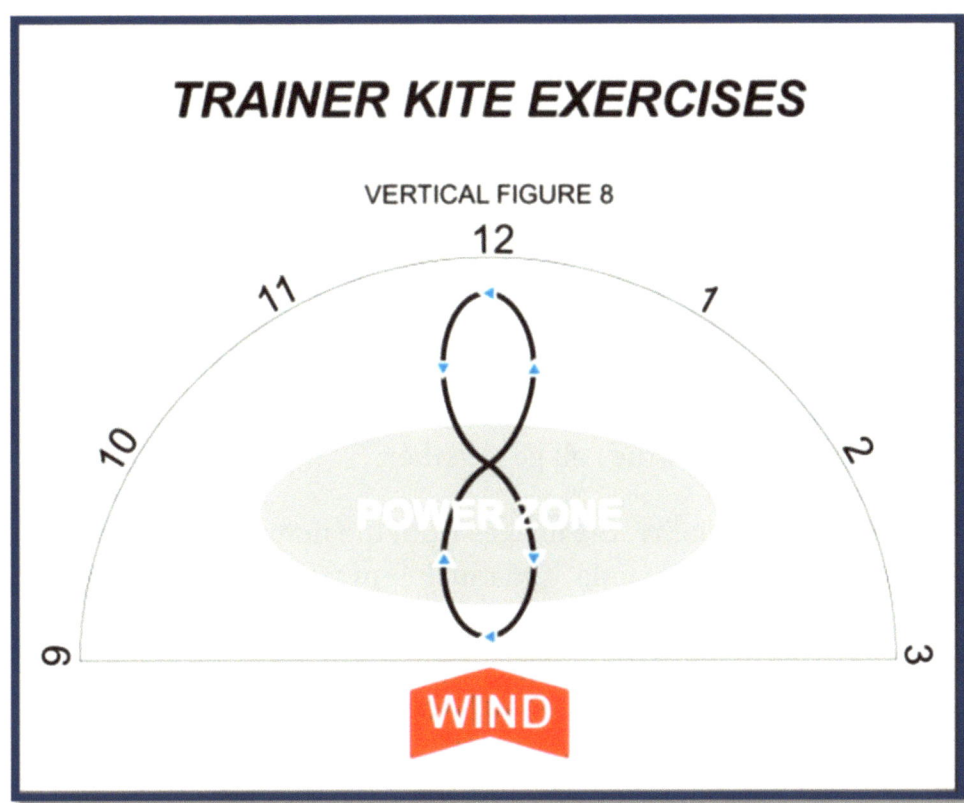

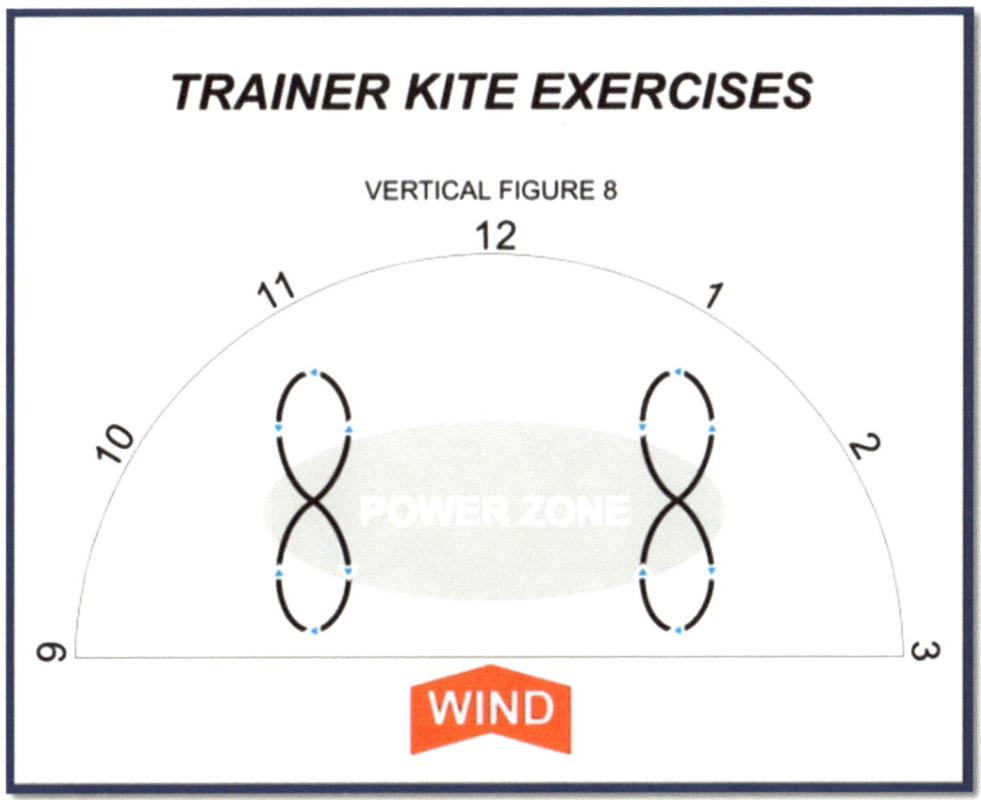

Know Your Equipment

Every piece of equipment is going to come with detailed instructions from the manufacturer that tells you exactly how to set it up. It is very important that you follow them carefully and not assume that one kite is like another. This is especially true of the bar set up.

The good folks at Wainman Hawaii® have allowed me to use the manuals for one of their Rabbit Kites and Carrot Bar here so that you can see in detail how the setup goes. If you use different equipment your details will vary, but this guide gives a great breakdown of the parts and how they all go together.

In order to retain print quality, the images from the manual could not be enlarged, but you can see the whole manual in much better detail at http://www.wainmanhawaii.com/manual.

The Package

When you buy a kite, this is what you will typically get:

4: Equipment Operation | **71**

The Kite

1. Thermo-molded bumpers – EVA foam
2. (Part A) Center line pigtail attachment point using larks head knot
2. (Part B) Ronstan Pulley
3. Rear (steering) line pigtail attachment points. The steering line pigtail comes set on the "STOCK" setting (no label) on the LE. To increase the turning speed of the kite, remove pigtail and re-attach to the FAST tab. To decrease the turning speed, re-attach the pigtail to the SLOW setting. The various turning speed options of the Rabbit combined with the bridle attachments can provide unique flying and bar pressure characteristics.
4. Steering line pigtail. Attach color-coded steering line to pigtail using larks head knot. The **LEFT** steering line and pigtail is **ORANGE**. The **RIGHT** steering line and pigtail is **GREEN**. There are (3) knots on the pigtail that you can attach the back line to: Strong Wind Knot, Center Knot, and Light Wind Knot. (See Rigging Tips.)

5. Center line bridle attachment options – changes flying characteristics.
6. (Part A) Leading Edge (LE) Inflate Valve
6. (Part B) LE Dump Valve
7. Strut inflation/deflation valve with strut deflater attachment
8. Single Line Attachment point options on LE for 5m. 6.5m, 7.5m, and 9m **Only.** See Single Line section.

Bridle Options

For the first few sessions, it is suggested that Rabbits are used on the factory "STOCK" setting. This setting is the bridle configuration that comes straight out of the bag when you purchase the kite (MIDDLE loop on the LE and knot on the LE pigtail).

Due to the low aspect ratio of the Rabbit canopy, the kite needs to be moved faster around the wind window to generate momentum. It is very important to properly trim the kite on the clam cleat. If the kite is not properly trimmed, the kite's performance may be jeopardized by back stalling and other problems.

When you decide it is time to change the Rabbit performance characteristics, it is suggested that you always make a single change at a time to the bridle and the back lines. This approach will enable the rider to find the perfect setting to match their riding style and get the best performance from her kite.

> **Remember:** When changing the bridle setting, be sure to adjust the knot to the corresponding setting:
>
> - UPWIND tab on LE/UPWIND knot on LE pigtail
> - DOWNWIND tab on LE/DOWNWIND knot on LE pigtail
> - "STOCK" tab (not labeled on kite) on LE/"STOCK" center knot on LE pigtail

Stock Setting

The Rabbit Kite Bridle comes out of the bag set to the "STOCK" setting – attached to the "STOCK" tab on the LE and the "STOCK" center knot on the LE pigtail. The bridle attaches to one of 3 knots on an LE pigtail.

As long as you pair the tabs with the corresponding knots, you are able to safely adjust the kite to the riding characteristic you want. These connections are easy to tell apart to minimize mistakes: UPWIND and DOWNWIND are prominently labeled, and "STOCK," the center knot, is not labeled.

The "STOCK" setting is the optimal all-round setting. You can adjust the bridle to find your favorite riding characteristic with the kite. To change the settings, unfasten the lark's head knot on the LE pigtail. Then, remove the LE pigtail and attach it to the desired tab (UPWIND or DOWNWIND). Just remember to make one change at a time to optimize your experience.

Upwind Setting

Attach the LE pigtail to the UPWIND tab on the LE. Attach the lark's head knot to the UPWIND knot (see diagram above) on the LE pigtail labeled UPWIND on the kite. This bridle option will make the kite shift further toward the edge of the wind window, enabling better upwind capabilities.

The kite will turn a bit "SLOW" compared to the "STOCK" setting, and it will jump a bit with a traditional vertical lift. This setting will also have increased bar pressure, which may take some getting used to.

Downwind Setting

Attach the LE pigtail to the DOWNWIND tab on the LE. Attach the lark's head knot to the DOWNWIND knot (see diagram above) on the LE pigtail labeled DOWNWIND on the kite. This bridle option will make the kite shift back into the window, increasing downwind riding.

The kite will turn faster than it will with the "STOCK" setting, and it will jump with a more horizontal lift. As the kite sits deeper (further back) in the window, it is a favorite for wave riding and for everyday light weight riders, since the bar pressure decreases.

"Boss" & "Big Mama" Bridles

The 12m "Boss" bridle and the 14.5m "Big Mama" bridle are double-V designs, whereas the 10.5m "Punch" bridle, the 9m "Smoke" bridle, the 7.5m "Mr. Green" bridle, the 6.25m "Gypsy" bridle, and 5m "Bunny" bridle feature compact-V designs.

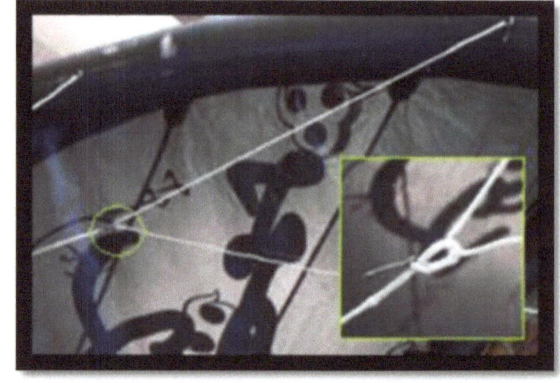

Remember: When changing a setting on the 12m and 14.5m "Boss" and "Big Mama" bridles, be sure to loosen the lark's head loop first (see diagram). After you have loosened the lark's head loop, it is very important that you get a proper and traditional launch from the edge of the wind window. This will ensure that the bridle will find the best setting. This should also be done periodically if you feel your kite pulling to one side (after ruling out uneven line lengths) since the loop can shift if you slam your kite down repeatedly.

Single Line Setups

Note: The single line attachment point option on the LE is available ONLY for 5m "Bunny" bridles, 6.25m "Gypsy" bridles, 7.5m "Mr. Green" bridles, and 9m "Smoke" bridles.

4: Equipment Operation | 75

To get a more direct feel and increased responsiveness in the kite, the 5M, 6.25M, 7.5M, and 9M Rabbits can ONLY be ridden without the "STOCK" bridle. This setting is called the Single Line setup. Start by removing the bridal from the LE of the kite. There are two SINGLE line attachment points on the LE.

Similar to the bridal options there is an UPWIND and DOWNWIND setting (not labeled on the kite). See Figure 2 and 3. Attach the SINGLE line pigtail (found in front pouch of the Rabbit Bag – Figure 1) to SINGLE tab of your choice.

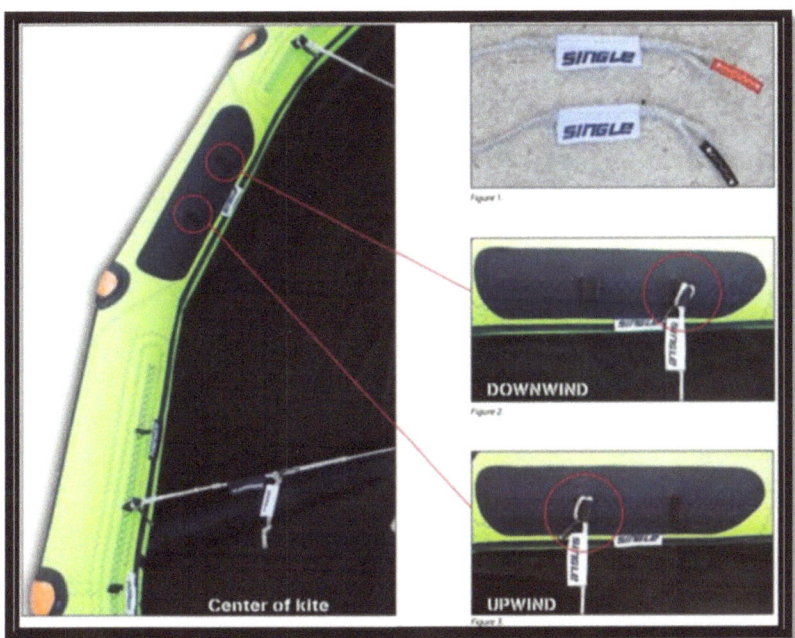

The SINGLE tab closest to the center of the kite is the UPWIND setting. After removing the bridle, attach the color-coded SINGLE line pigtail(s) to the tab(s). Attach center line to pigtail using lark's head knot. This will give similar characteristics to the UPWIND bridle options.

The SINGLE tab furthest from the center of the kite is the DOWNWIND SINGLE setting. After removing the bridle, attach the color-coded SINGLE line pigtail(s) to the tab(s). Attach center line to pigtail using lark's head knot. This will give similar characteristics as the DOWNWIND bridle options.

SINGLE line is recommended for advanced riders only as the kite will be less forgiving of errors and will have a super "FAST" turning speed. The SINGLE line will have similar depower capabilities as the Rabbit with the bridle/pulley. The SINGLE line setting works optimally for riders up to 165 pounds. Make sure that the kite is very well inflated.

HowToKiteSurf.com

Rigging Tips

> **REMEMBER: Safety is the number one priority.** As mentioned before, it is VERY IMPORTANT that you take lessons with a competent and certified instructor which will ensure safe kite setup and rigging.

Below are a few steps on rigging the Rabbit.

STEP 1. There are two ways of laying out your lines – upwind and downwind of the kite. We highly recommend rigging DOWNWIND of the kite. There will be certain situations that you can only lay out your lines upwind of the kite.

When rigging DOWNWIND, make sure that your bar is placed upside down and green rear line is on the left and orange rear line is on the right. Separate all four lines by combining the lines toward the kite with the green line on your left and orange on the right. Double-check that no lines are crossed over each other.

STEP 2. Once you have pumped up your kite (see tips section), separated all four lines, and double-checked that no lines are crossed over each other, you can attach the lines to the pigtails on the kite. The lines are color coded to ensure that you attach the correct lines to the corresponding pigtail on the kite.

◇◇◇ Tips From Tyson ◇◇◇

Stomp the bar into the sand/snow to give it some resistance so that when you run out your lines, you don't drag the bar. Keep the outside lines/steering lines on the outside of your legs and the inside lines/front lines in between your legs.

I like to lay out my lines first, then place the kite over the lines. Also, before I hook my back lines up, I always do a spot check and lift up the line to make sure it goes all the way back to the bar and is not tangled within any of the other lines.

◇◇◇

4: Equipment Operation | 77

Attaching Rear Steering Lines:

Attach figure 8 steering line to pigtail using lark's head knot. The **LEFT** steering line and pigtail is **ORANGE**. The **RIGHT** steering line and pigtail is **GREEN**.

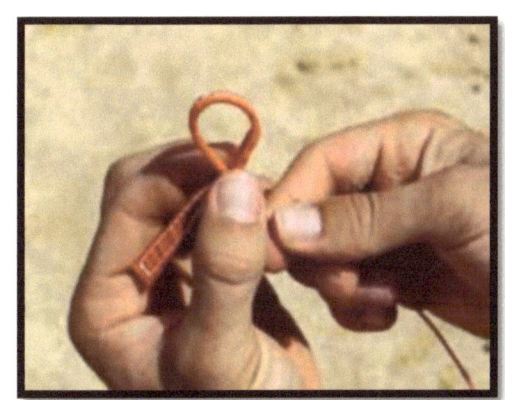

Depending on the wind conditions and rider experience level, always start by using the MIDDLE knot and move it up or down to get more or less power.

There are (3) knots on the pigtail that you can attach the back line to. They are:

Strong Wind – The knot (furthest from the kite) will lengthen the back lines by providing more depower capabilities. This setting is recommended when you are over powered and need to spill extra power from the kite.

Recommended Knot

Center Knot – This knot provides power in the kite that is in between Strong Wind and Light Wind.

Light Wind – The knot closest to the kite will shorten the back lines and provide the most power in your kite.

NOTE: When adjusting the position of the rear line pigtail ("SLOW" or "FAST") at the webbing on the kite tips, the rear to center line length ratio will also change. Please make sure your kite is trimmed correctly to ensure that the kite does not over sheet or back stall.

Attaching Front Center Lines:

Attach color-coded **GREY** and labeled **CENTER** line to the pigtail that is labeled **CENTER** (it is attached to the pulley) using lark's head knot. See the picture to the left.

There are two knots on the pigtail. Make sure you use the same knot on each side and that the pulley is free of sand and dirt and that it is turning freely on the bridle line.

You can use 2 different knots in situations where your center lines are not of equal length. This is only a temporary solution, and if your front lines are not equal, they must be adjusted.

STEP 3. Once you have attached your lines, once again be sure to do a final check to make sure that your lines are connected to the corresponding pigtails and that they are not crossed. Make sure all knots are on their corresponding pigtail.

STEP 4. If you have rigged your kite for DOWNWIND, **DO NOT FORGET** to flip your bar over the correct way (DANGER label on the bar facing down; left hand on the orange side; right hand on green side). Double-check once again to make sure that your lines are not crossed before you hook your harness loop into the spreader bar.

Carrot Bar Equipment Diagram

1. **FLYING LINES:**

    A. FRONT FLYING LINES: 330kg/725lbs. grey color lines with preassembled extensions that can be removed for different kite flying characteristics.

    B. REAR FLYING LINES: 220kg/485lbs orange & green color-coded lines with preassembled extensions that can be removed for different kite-flying characteristics.

2. **SWIVEL WITH CERAMIC BEARING:** Marine swivel with the breaking strain of 500kg/1100lbs. This unique high performance ceramic bearing offers unmatched free-spinning capabilities under high tension loads without any corrosion or other risks that could result in the swivel getting stuck. This swivel allows for multiple safety set-up options and easy maintenance.

3. **RELAUNCH BALL:** The relaunch balls on the back lines are used to assist in relaunching the kite when the leading edge is down. Grab the relaunch ball in windy conditions, and pull toward you to help re-launch the kite.

4. **POWER TRIM ADJUSTMENT WITH MAGIC VELCRO®:** Simple trimming system based on the original Calm Cleat mechanism. Pull the rope in to shorten the front lines and reduce the kite's power, or slacken the rope to lengthen front lines and increase power. The strong Velcro® strip keeps the extra adjustment rope in place while riding.

5. **SOFT BAR ENDS AND COMFORT BAR GRIP:** Ergonomic molded EVA (floating cushy foam) bar ends provide soft grip texture while riding, and they float the bar when it's in the water. The line winder and integrated bungees on the bar ends keep the wound lines in place after the flight is over. Molded "BMX" bar grip provides extra comfort for your hands while steering your kite.

6. **CUSTOM DEPOWER LINE**: Dimmed transparent PU (very strong plastic) tube

with two separate compartments, the tube houses the depower main line (600kg/1320lbs of breaking strain) and safety bungee line. This combo is perfectly fitted in the center hole of the bar, providing superb power/depower capabilities and results in amazingly responsive kite performance.

7. SAFETY BUFFER: This unique buffer solution provides functionality for different safety setup options. The buffer length also ensures that all quick release activations will be successful! Additionally, the buffer provides chicken loop stability for unhooked riding as it gently locks into the center hole of the bar.

8. SAFETY QUICK RELEASE: The push away quick release handle is used to protect the kite and the rider in emergency situations. Depending on the selected set-up option, the kite will significantly depower, totally depower (flag), or completely separate from the rider.

9. SOFT HARNESS LOOP: Covered with molded EVA (soft cushy foam), the harness loop is extremely easy on the hands, plus it floats in the water. Due to its construction, the loop doesn't elongate while riding. It comes equipped with a

removable security pin (Dingy Guy), and the small, integrated ring can be used as a leash attachment point for "One Release" set-up.

Carrot Bar Stock Set-Up

The "STOCK" set-up is how the bar comes "out of the bag" and is geared toward the everyday rider that engages the safety quick release only in rare emergency situations. With this option, you attach the bar leash to the "safety" ring located on the buffer of the "STOCK" bar.

When the quick release is engaged in an emergency, the bar leash will stay connected to one of the front lines and "flag" the kite (depowers the kite 100%). If you're still in danger, activate your safety quick release on the safety leash to totally separate from the kite.

> *IMPORTANT:* Always attach clip (closest to red release) to your harness so you can reach the release when needed.

Carrot Bar: Suicide Connection Set-Up

The "Suicide Connection" set-up is for experienced riders only. It may meet the needs of expert riders who like to show off on the waves but don't want to lose their kite. It allows for unhooked riding and letting go of the bar without kite "flagging," even if you activate the quick release.

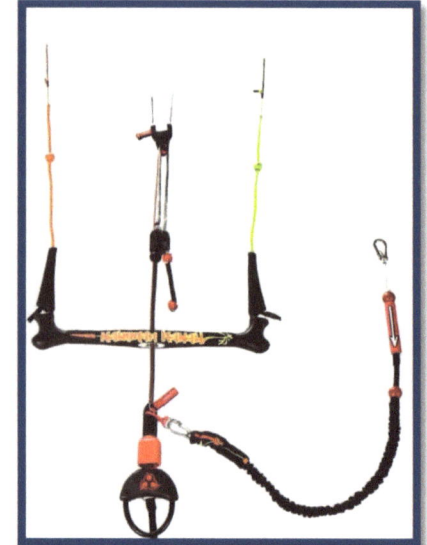

After you convert the bar to "Suicide Connection" by attaching the suicide connector to the buffer, attach the safety leash to the ring on the suicide connector. When you unhook and let go of the bar, the kite will depower for the distance of the depower main line.

If you activate your quick release, you will still be attached to the kite by the safety leash, and you must activate the safety leash in order to release the kite. If a situation requires that you need to "flag" your kite, grab the safety buffer handle prior to activating the release on the leash.

HOW TO PREPARE A SUICIDE CONNECTION:

You MUST have a suicide connector metal ring to rig your suicide connection.

1. Remove the suicide connector and ring from the Carrot Bar accessory bag.

2. Feed the suicide connector through the hole in the buffer.

4: Equipment Operation | **83**

3. Loop the suicide connector around the buffer.

4. Feed both ends of the suicide connector through the loop.

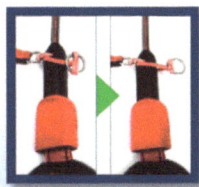

5. Attach the ring to the suicide connector as illustrated above.

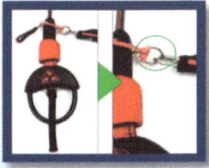

6. Attach your safety leash to the suicide connector on both the buffer (shown above) and your harness.

> **IMPORTANT:** Always attach clip (closest to red release) to your harness so you can reach the release when needed.

Carrot Bar: Double Depower Set-Up

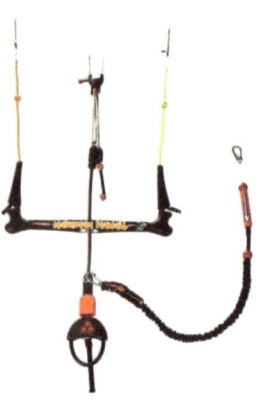

The "Double Depower" setup is for experienced riders only, and it's a favorite among avid freestylers. It allows for unhooked riding and releasing.

After you convert the bar to the "Double Depower" set-up, attach the safety leash to the ring on the buffer. Activating the double depower (by unhooking and releasing the bar) shortens your center lines to twice the distance of the depower main line. If you activate your quick release, you will still be attached to the kite by the safety leash, and you must activate the safety leash in order to release the kite.

HOW TO PREPARE A DOUBLE DEPOWER SET-UP:

You MUST have a front line swivel connector and a metal ring to rig a Double Depower set-up. In addition, an extra supply of thin line is needed.

1. Remove the Safety Ring from the red bungee.

2. Attach thin line to the bungee.

3. Pull the bungee through the plastic tube.

4. Remove the thin line from the bungee.

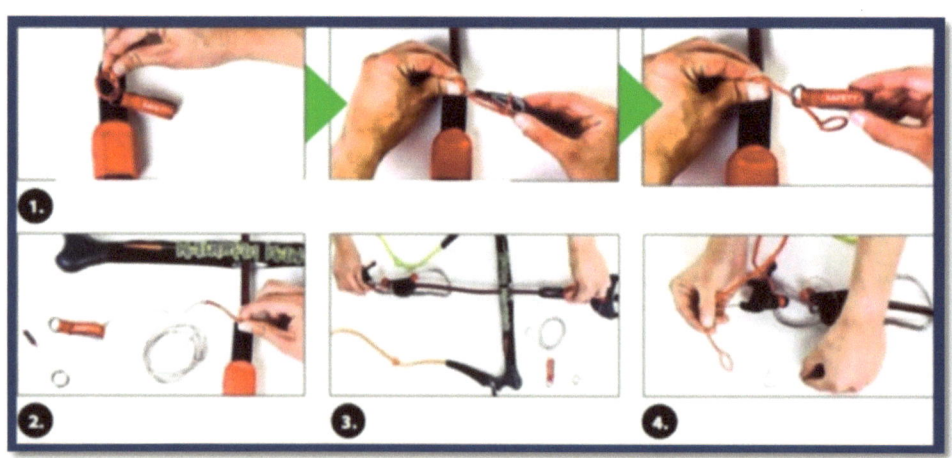

5. Pull the bungee through the swivel and remove the front (gray) center line from the bungee. Do not pull gray front line through the swivel.

6. Locate the front line (red) swivel connector in Carrot Bar accessory bag.

7. Attach the red connector to the gray front lines.

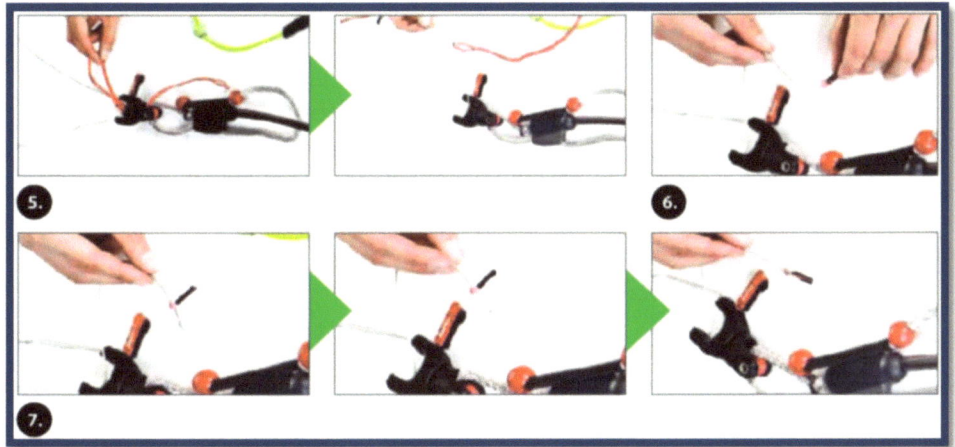

8. Once the connector is attached to front line, pull it tight as it seats firmly in the swivel.

9. Feed the bungee line through the side hole of swivel and loop through itself.

10. Attach the thin line to the bungee.

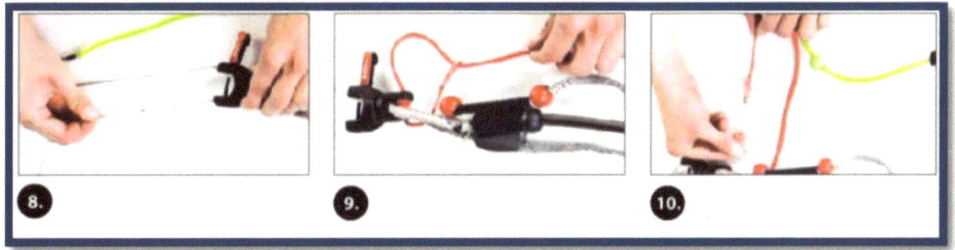

11. Pull the bungee back through the plastic tube.

12. Remove the thin line from bungee.

13. Locate the metal ring in Carrot Bar accessory bag.

14. Attach the metal ring to the bungee as illustrated above.

15. Attach your safety leash to the metal ring (shown above) and your harness.

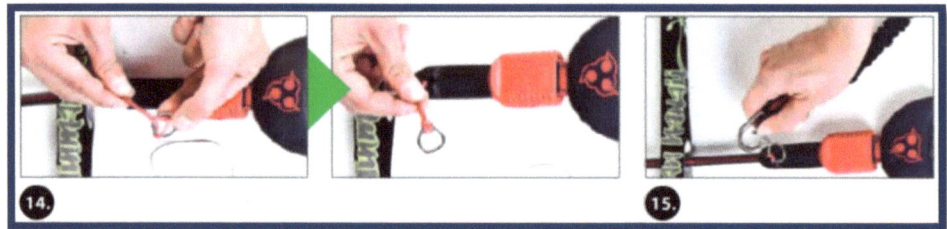

Carrot Bar: School Safety Set-Up

The "School Safety" set-up is geared toward beginners and all other riders that want the safest option while riding. It provides the least wear/tear on the bar components and the smoothest flag out activation.

This setup is ideal for kite schools and for kiters that engage the quick release regularly. This is the safest riding method due to the complete power loss when "flagging" the kite on one of the front lines in an emergency situation.

HOW TO PREPARE A SCHOOL SAFETY SET-UP:

Find the School Safety Line. It's the grey line and red sleeve in the accessory bag. Also gather the Front Line Swivel labeled "Safety."

1. Remove the extension from the gray center line that is connected to the red bungee.

2. After removing the extension, pull the center line attached to bungee through the swivel.

3. Remove the center line from the bungee.

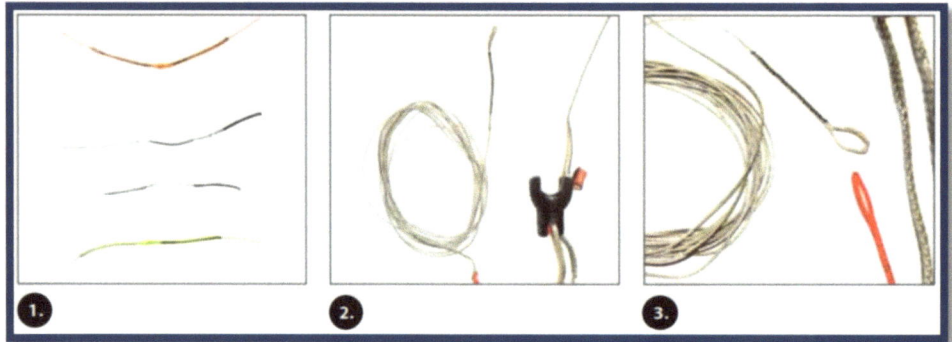

4. Feed the center line back through the swivel and attach "Safety" labeled connector.

5. Feed the bungee through the center of the swivel.

6. Connect the "Safety Line" to the red bungee.

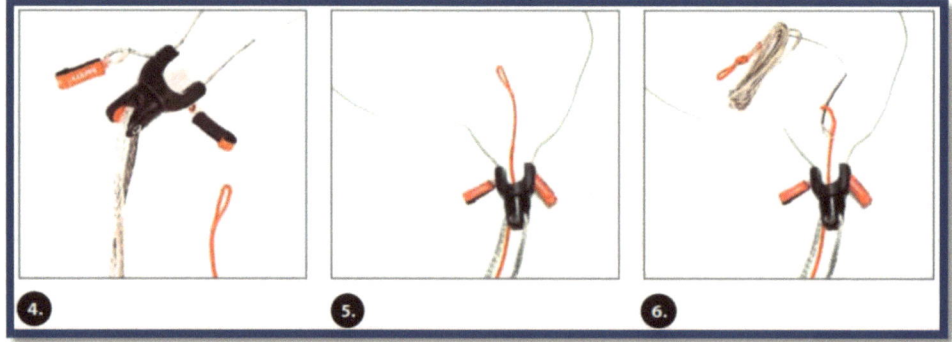

7. Connect the "Safety" and center line to the extension that was originally removed.

8. Attach your safety leash to the metal ring (with safety label) and your harness.

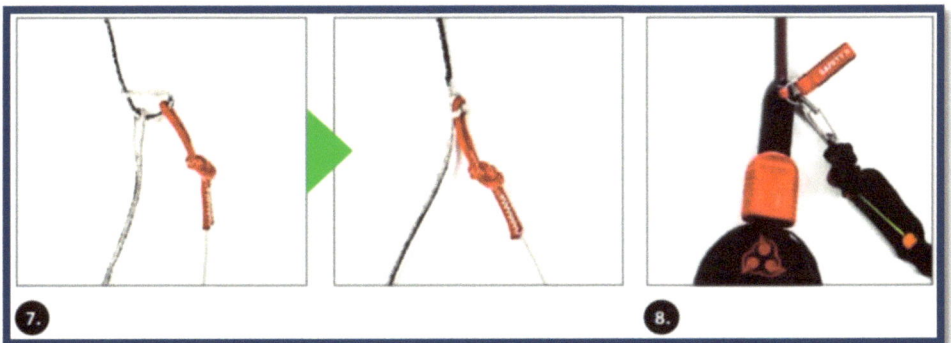

Carrot Bar: One Release Set-Up

The "One Release" set-up is based on the simple principle that in case of immediate and serious danger, there should be one ultimate kite release where the kite will be completely detached from the rider. When choosing this setup, you have to be aware that when you activate your QR, your kite will fly away and you may never get it back.

Make sure you aren't riding upwind from anyone when activating the QR to avoid harming anyone downwind from you. "One Release" can be ridden with the "Dingy Guy" or without it.

Attach the safety leash to the metal ring on the harness loop (where the security pin labeled "Dingy Guy" is attached). When you unhook and release the bar, the kite will depower for the distance of the depower main line. If you activate your quick release, you will be completely separated from the kite. In certain circumstances, you may have time to grab the Safety Handle on the buffer while activating the QR, which

4: Equipment Operation | 91

will flag out the kite on one of the front lines.

HOW TO PREPARE A ONE RELEASE SET-UP:

Attach your safety leash to the ring on the harness loop and to your harness.

> *IMPORTANT:* Always attach clip (closest to red release) to your harness so you can reach the release when needed.

The Quick Release & Safety Leash

Please remember that it is always your (and others') health and life that is more important than the kite itself. If you ever feel that you are in a dangerous and uncertain situation, **activate the quick release**. Be logical, know your limits, and kite in a safe environment.

> *NOTE:* After every session, the quick release on both the harness loop and safety leash should be rinsed with fresh water. Before every session, the quick release should be checked for solid functionality or it should be replaced.

ACTIVATING THE QUICK RELEASE:

> REMEMBER: It is always your (and others) health and life that is more important than the kite itself. If you ever feel that you are in a dangerous and uncertain situation, **activate the quick release.** Be logical, know your limits, and kite responsibly in a safe environment.

Every rider should be thoroughly familiar with activating the Quick Release in emergencies.

To activate your Quick Release, please follow steps below:

HowToKiteSurf.com

1. Grab Quick Release firmly.

2. Push Quick Release hard away from yourself (in direction of arrow).

3. The Quick Release then pushes against the tension, and it will separate the kite from the harness loop.

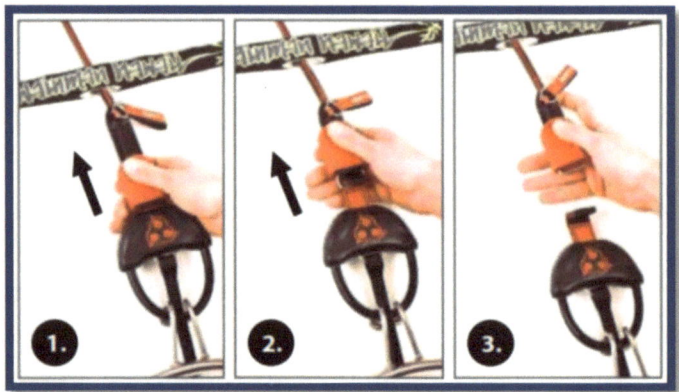

RESETTING THE QUICK RELEASE:

To reset the Quick Release, please follow steps below:

1. Slide lip of Harness Loop through the metal rectangle (below Quick Release).

2. Bend the lip down, grab the Quick Release, and pull toward yourself (in opposite direction of arrow).

3. Keep pulling (toward you) until Quick Release mechanism "snaps" into place.

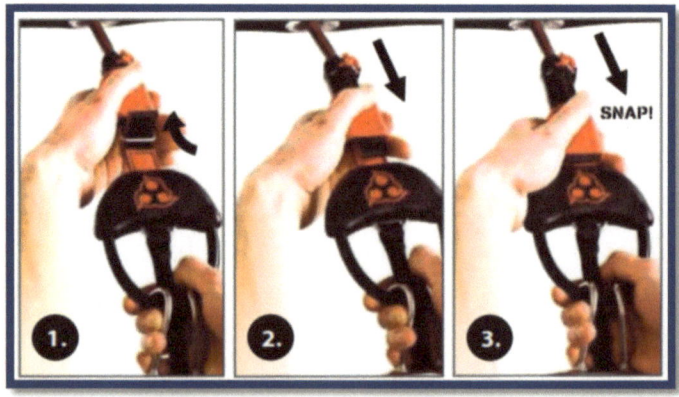

THE SAFETY LEASH:

> **IMPORTANT:** Always attach the clip (closest to red release) to your harness so you can reach the release when needed. The other clip will be attached to one of the places described in the Carrot Bar section.

RELEASING THE SAFETY LEASH:

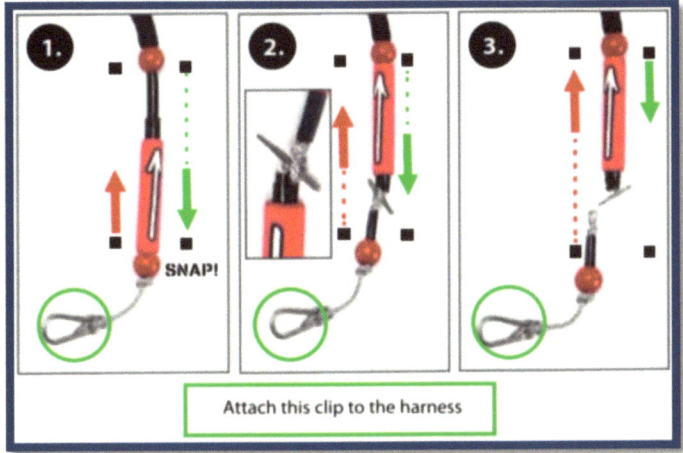

To activate the safety leash release, grab the red handle firmly and push handle away from yourself in the direction of the red arrow.

RESETTING THE SAFETY LEASH:

To reset the safety leash, slide the metal pin through the loop, turn, and pull it toward yourself (green arrow) until it "snaps" into place.

Tips & Info

> **REMEMBER:** Safety is the number one priority.

1. While setting up your kite before every session, always make sure that your swivel and pulley move freely and are not jammed.

2. You should frequently check your flying lines to ensure that **all 4 lines** are equal in length when the bar is trimmed at full power. To check them, release the depower rope out of clan cleat. Flying lines will typically stretch with use over time. Check with your local shop about line stretching/adjusting techniques.

3. Check your bridle rope (where the pulley runs on) for frays and weak points. Your bridle will have normal wear and tear over time, and it should be regularly replaced to avoid bridle snapping while riding.

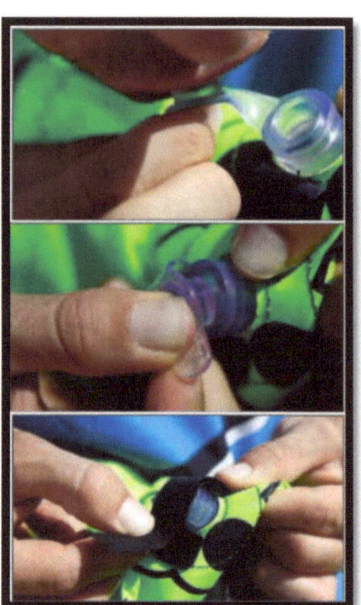

4. You should frequently inspect your kite canopy for small holes and check the seams for fraying. It is a good habit to inspect these areas while you are pumping your kite.

5. Make sure your lines are free of knots, tangles, and any damage while setting up and/or de-rigging your lines.

6. When closing the deflation valve on the LE, remember to wet it, snap it, and shut and seal it tightly with Velcro®.

7. After using the strut deflater attachment (pin), it is very important that you DO NOT leave the pin in the valve when packing the kite away.

8. Use Magic Velcro® to secure any dangling depower rope to prevent tangling.

9. Remember to trim your kite with your depower rope/clam cleat for optimal performance. Failure to do so may result in the kite over- or under-sheeting. Check with your local kite shop or instructor for trimmer techniques.

10. Make sure you have the right kite with the right bar:

    • The 5m & 6.25m uses a Small bar (21.5m lines).

    • The 7.5m, 9m, &10m uses a Medium bar (23m lines).

- The 12m & 14.5m uses a Large bar (24.5m lines).

11. Secure your kite on the beach at all times (using sand, compression bag filled with sand, etc.) to prevent it from flying away and possibly hurting someone.

12. Pump the kite "right," but be cautious to not over-inflate it.

13. Certain situations will cause the kite to invert, such as when the kite is rolled over by waves. To get the kite to revert back upright, let go of the bar and swim hard toward the kite while pushing it over.

14. Always rinse the swivel after every session and ensure that it spins freely.

15. Make sure you inspect your flying lines on the swivel, following the instructions. The lines pass though the swivel regularly during use, and that puts them under a bigger threat of breaking if  the system is frequently activated. This is standard wear and tear on the lines, and you have to inspect them before every session and replace them if needed.

Riding toe side

Chapter 4 FAQs & Common Misconceptions

Q: Can I use a foil trainer kite when I'm going to ultimately be using an inflatable?

A: Foil trainer kites are great. You can save money by getting a simpler kite, but you still get the experience of flying the kite and learning how to control it. There will be differences between the feel of the trainer and a "real" kite, but that would be true if they were both inflatables too.

Chapter 5: Techniques

Ready to Launch?

Be sure that the person that helps you launch your kite has been properly trained. She should hold the kite at 6:00 or 9:00 with the leading edge facing upwind.

Choose a wide-open space free of obstacles and people to set up.

5: Techniques | 99

Always double- and triple-check your kite and gear before going out on the water. Ask for help if you think something is wrong.

Walk upwind while the assistant rotates downwind, keeping the lines extended. Watch your kite and walk until you see that it stops flapping. Walk back downwind, again with the assistant keeping the kite extended, until you get to a point where the kite is stable and just about hovers by itself.

Do a last-minute check of your gear, and give the thumbs-up signal to launch.

When the assistant lets go of the kite it will stay where it is, and you can slowly pilot it to the top of the wind window.

◊◊◊ **Tips From Tyson** ◊◊◊

Before I give the thumbs up for a launch, I always think "outback." I do this to remind me to make sure that my back lines are on the outside, and clear of, any others. It's very important that both the steering lines/back lines are clear and go straight to the kite.

◊◊◊

Give the thumbs-up to signal you are ready for the kite to be launched and everything is OKAY.

Always do a final check of your lines, safety leash, harness and kite before giving the "thumbs-up."

Assisted Landing

When you are ready to land your kite, pat your head to signal that you are ready to land and see that your assistant signals back. Lower the kite and when your assistant grabs the leading edge, take a few steps towards him. The assistant should then lay the kite in the sand.

Assisted Landing

Self-Launch

Self-launching is not recommended and can result in serious injury. If for some reason you must launch your kite alone, make sure that there is no one near the kite.

Do not allow untrained people to assist your launch because they could get hurt.

Check that all your gear is correctly set up. Lay out your kite, top side down with the lines extended perpendicular to the direction the wind is blowing. Then walk your bar upwind of the kite, allowing the lines to make an arc. Bend the upwind wingtip over and weigh it down with sand.

Take hold of your control bar and as the wind fills the kite, walk backwards. As the kite catches the wind, the wingtip will flip back down and you can pilot the kite.

Point the kite to the wind and secure the kite with sand before attaching the lines to the kite.

5: Techniques | 103

Never kite alone.

Self-Landing

Self-landing is not recommended for beginners, but if you must, the best way to do it is to depower over the water and allow the kite to slowly fall in the water, just as you would to begin a self rescue.

Relaunching

◊◊◊ **Tips From Tyson** ◊◊◊

Water relaunching the kite is one of the more finesse-oriented aspects of the sport.

The smaller the kite, and stronger the wind, the easier it's going to be.

Especially with a larger, higher-aspect kite in light winds, keep in mind that once the kite has rotated and moved to where a wingtip is now the only part of the kite on the water, you don't want to keep as much tension on the steering line. Because the kite is large, you need more pressure for it to turn and create lift. Once the kite is on its side and moving towards the edge of the wind window, maintain less tension on the steering line, allow for the water to drain from between the leading edge and canopy slowly so that the kite can come up off the water. You want to avoid having the kite stall and fall back into the water on its trailing edge.

◇◇◇

How to Perform a Rabbit Relaunch

> **REMEMBER: Safety is the number one priority.** It is **VERY IMPORTANT** that you take lessons with a competent and certified instructor which will ensure safe kite relaunch. Make sure your kite is properly inflated which will assist in easy and quick relaunch capability.
> **REMEMBER:** Safety is the number one priority.

Before making a rabbit re-launch, make sure that your kite is properly inflated to ensure a fast and easy re-launch and follow the steps below:

STEP 1. When the kite and the leading edge go down into the water, make sure the kite is directly downwind of you. To make sure that your lines are not crossing each other, flip the bar upside down and spin it until the lines are uncrossed. Try to keep your board on your feet since the added resistance that the board provides will assist in quicker relaunch.

 **STEP 2.** Remember that the bar will now be flipped over, so once you have uncrossed the lines, spin the bar to face right side up, grab one of the rear lines (a Relaunch Ball can help a lot), and pull it toward your body as illustrated. This will cause the wind to catch the sail and the wing tip to lift.

STEP 3. Once the wing tip lifts, the kite will rotate on its side and start moving toward the wind window. Remember to keep the bar tension high to maintain rear line tension

5: Techniques | 105

and to aim the bar toward the side of the wind window that you are trying to reach.

STEP 4. Keep the tension on the line as the kite moves toward the edge of the window on its wing tip. Now it's ready for relaunch.

STEP 5. As the kite starts to relaunch, level out your bar and slowly direct the kite up into the sky. Remember to sheet the bar out to depower the kite as soon as the kite leaves the water.

HowToKiteSurf.com

How to Perform a Traditional Relaunch

> **REMEMBER: Safety is the number one priority.** It is **VERY IMPORTANT** that you take lessons with a competent and certified instructor to ensure that you can consistently and safely execute a kite relaunch. Make sure your kite is properly inflated to assist in a quick and easy relaunch.

Depending on the wind conditions and other variables such as currents, it may take a little extra effort to get the kite on its wing tip and to the edge of the wind window. You may have to use the relaunch method as illustrated above. This concept is very similar to the simple relaunch previously described, but it requires letting go of the board and swimming toward the kite.

STEP 1. When the kite and the leading edge go down into the water, make sure the kite is directly downwind from you. To make sure that your lines are not crossing each other, spin the bar until the lines are uncrossed. Flip the bar over into the correct position. Swim toward your kite to flip it over on its back. The picture shows kite on its LE. Be sure to keep tension in the lines, and do not swim too close to the kite or it will flip back onto its top.

STEP 2. Once the kite is almost on its back, grab a rear line, the Relaunch Ball can help with this, and pull it toward your body. This will cause the wind to catch the sail and make the wing tip lift.

STEP 3. Once the wing tip lifts, the kite will rotate on its side and start moving toward the wind window. Push the bar all the way out and reach past the

bar and pull on the outside/steering line until the kite is on a wing tip. Once it has rotated onto its wingtip, maintain tension (but not enough to make it flip. Try and allow the kite to lift up off the water slowly, being careful not to steer the kite too aggressively. Allow it to come up slowly so that you don't get pulled too much and get separated from your board.

STEP 4. Keep the bar sheeted in, and keep the kite moving to the edge of the window on its wing tip. Now it's ready for relaunch.

STEP 5. As the kite starts to relaunch, level out your bar and slowly direct the kite up into the sky. Remember to sheet the bar out to depower the kite once it leaves the water.

Pull one outside line to relaunch kite.

Body Dragging

When you lose your board in the water, you will often need to get upwind to recover it. The technique you use is body dragging. This is a "superman" float on your stomach in the water, using your kite to pull you where you want to go. Stay on your belly with one arm holding your kite at 45 degrees from the ground and your other arm extended toward the upwind direction of your tack. You may need to tack a short distance and then switch arms and tack the other way to get far enough. Body dragging is also used to get to shore or when you just need to move in the water.

Body drag upwind to retrieve your board

Getting Up on the Board

The waterstart is the most common way to get up on the board. Start in a sitting position in the water with your board on your feet in front of you. Dive the kite into the power zone and as it pulls, keep the bar in front of your body (don't let your arms swing overhead). As the kite starts to lift you, keep your rear knee bent and put your weight on your back foot, pulling it under your center as you start to straighten your front leg and use it to direct the board downwind.

Self-Rescue

It's very important that you know what to do if you get stranded out in the water. Getting yourself back to shore with your kite when you can't even coast in by body dragging is called self-rescue, and it is something you must practice before you find yourself needing the skills. It's a bit involved, and you need to be proficient at it so you don't wear yourself out trying to figure out what to do.

Body drag away from the shore before putting on your board

Why would you need to self-rescue? There are two primary reasons – wind problems and equipment failure.

Sometimes the wind just stops, and you may find yourself a long distance from shore with no wind to get you back in. Another possibility is that the wind can change to an offshore wind, and you need to keep your kite down to avoid the risk of being dragged out to sea.

Equipment failure could result from an incident in which your kite gets damaged, but the most common cause is "operator error," particularly with inflatable kites. When you inflate your kite, be sure to follow manufacturer's instructions and close off any valves that separate the baffles. If you have Velcro® tabs over the fill-valves, be sure those are properly closed to assure that your valves don't get opened and allow the kite to deflate.

But say something has happened and you can't kite back to shore. Depending on the situation, there are three possible techniques available to you. All three will require you to get your kite in the water.

How to Recover Your Kite

Depower: If your kite is still in the air, depower it by using your emergency release to open the chicken loop. This causes your kite to flag on one of the front lines, and it will fall into the water. Make sure the kite doesn't accidentally launch by....

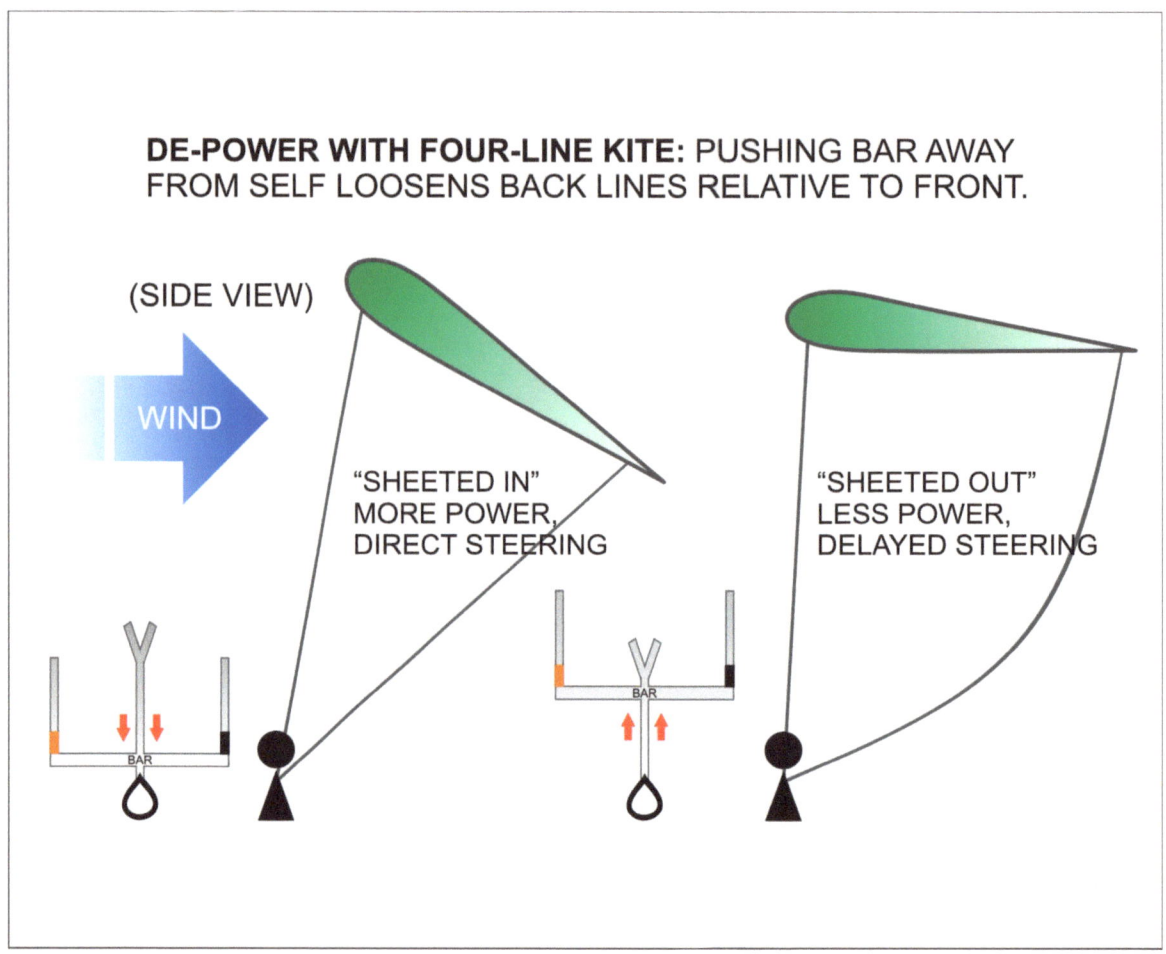

Retrieving Your Kite: Take hold of one of your front lines, and pull yourself toward the kite using either a hand-over-hand motion or by pulling in about a foot at a time until you reach the bar.

Wind the line around the bar, being careful to keep your feet and legs free of the other lines while you do this. It's during times like these that you are most likely to need a kite knife; should you get tangled in a line, you can simply cut it. Don't exhaust yourself trying to manage lines in deep water. If necessary, just cut the line and sort it out later.

After you have wrapped the first 20-30 feet of your front line around the bar to keep the kite from accidentally relaunching, begin wrapping the remaining lines around the ends of the bar. Continue to wrap the lines as you get nearer to the kite. When you are about half-a-kite length away, use a simple knot to tie the lines down on the bar.

Wind up your lines, and swim to your kite when doing a self rescue. Help others in need.

> **Safety Alert:** If the wind does somehow power up your kite during this process, just let go of everything. You are vulnerable to being injured by the lines, which can cut right through your skin with the power of a flying kite behind them. Don't take any chances.

Once you have your kite, there are three techniques you can use, depending on the circumstances and the wind direction.

Self-Rescue in Onshore or Side Onshore Winds

If your inflatable kite is still inflated and the wind is moving toward shore, you can use the kite to pull you in. Grab the center of the leading edge, and if your kite is flexible enough, fold it in half and grab the center line bridles on each end. If the kite is not flexible enough to do that, slide your hands down to one end and hold the wing tip between your knees while you slide your hands along the leading edge, bending the kite as you go, until you have reached the other end and can get the bridles in hand.

Position the kite with one wingtip in the water and the other up above, and turn so that the kite catches the wind and sails you in to shore. Be sure to practice this in shallow water so you get the hang of it before you have to do it in a real self-rescue situation. You may find that you have to switch the end that is in the water to change the side the leading edge is on if you are being taken in the wrong direction. Again, practice ahead of time so you know what to expect.

Self-Rescue in Offshore Winds

When the wind is trying to blow you out to sea, you will not be able to self-rescue by using the kite as a sail. In this case you will have to swim in, preferably using your kite as a raft. You may also need to go a short distance upwind to retrieve your board, and the first raft technique can be used for that.

Open Kite Raft: This simple raft technique is most desirable because it keeps the kite inflated and also makes you the most visible to rescue personnel. Once you have gotten back to your kite and tied your lines on the bar, lay on top of the kite with the leading edge under your upper chest. The wing tips will be out to your sides and will stick up in the air. The kite provides flotation for you as you swim it in to shore.

Bundled Kite Raft: If the leading edge is damaged or if the offshore wind is too strong to swim on top of the kite, deflate the leading edge but keep the struts inflated. (Be sure to close the deflate valve so you don't fill the bladder with water.) Roll the wingtips in and wrap your harness around the kite to keep it bundled. Lie on top of the "raft" and paddle back to shore.

How to Perform a Self-Rescue

> **REMEMBER: Safety is the number one priority**. Below are steps and tips on self-rescue. It is **VERY IMPORTANT** that you take lessons with a competent and certified instructor to make sure that you can safely perform a self-rescue.

Various circumstances may occur that require a self-rescue (high offshore winds, sudden and severe wind and weather conditions, broken equipment, and many other hazards you may encounter). Every rider should be well trained in proper self-rescue techniques. This self-rescue procedure applies to "School Safety" or "STOCK" set-ups, and it is effective for most emergency situations.

STEP 1. Activate the Quick Release on the harness loop. Since the bar is in either the "School Safety" or "STOCK" set up, the kite will depower and "flag" on the center line.

STEP 2. Take the ONE center line that you flagged the kite with and slowly start pulling yourself toward the kite until you have reached the bar. When you have the bar in hand, start wrapping the center line around the bar.

Once you have wrapped approximately 12-15 ft. of line around the bar, start wrapping the remaining three lines around the bar. This is to prevent your kite from accidentally powering up. While you wrap the lines, you should be slowly pulling yourself toward the depowered kite.

It can be difficult to avoid sometimes, but make sure you do NOT get tangled in your lines while wrapping them. It is recommended to always keep a kite knife with you in case you get tangled in your lines. Always watch the kite when winding up your lines, and be prepared to immediately drop everything if the wind increases and your kite gets powered up.

STEP 3. Once you have rolled up your lines to within half of the kite's length, tie the lines to the bar using a simple knot.

STEP 4. Grab the kite by the center of the leading edge and fold it in half. Keep folding until you reach the wing tips, and then grab the center line bridles.

STEP 5. If the wind leads you back to shore, position the kite in the direction of the wind and ride the kite back in.

STEP 6. Sail with the kite until you reach the beach or another safe location. Be sure that you secure your kite on the beach with sand bags or by covering it with sand to prevent it from blowing away and possibly injuring someone.

> **Note:** There are some instances where this self-rescue method is not effective, such as in offshore winds, violent winds, or when you have broken gear. If this is the case, first follow Steps 1-4.

Once you have secured the kite, deflate the leading edge (but *not* the struts) and roll up the kite. Secure it by wrapping your harness around it. Close the deflate valve afterwards so the bladder does not fill with water. Thanks to the still-inflated struts, the rolled kite will give you a makeshift flotation device so you can paddle back to shore.

After a self rescue, your lines will look like this!

Avoid Getting Lofted

"Getting lofted" means being lifted straight up into the air, and it can be very dangerous. Kiters have been suddenly lifted 200 feet into the air before returning to earth (or water) when the wind released them. It doesn't always work that way. Even if the kiter isn't just dropped like a stone, the fall is still fast and difficult to control. Needless to say, the situation should be avoided.

Avoid Getting Lofted

Lofting occurs in gusty and irregular winds when your kite is at or near the top of the wind window. The primary way to avoid it is to only kite in stable atmospheric conditions. Don't kite if you have gusty winds, see thunder clouds, or are having weather that is changing rapidly. The squall at the front of an approaching storm is the most likely cause of gusts, so even the arrival of a regular afternoon rain can be dangerous because the changing temperature as it comes off the water and hits land results in big changes in the wind. Lofting has occurred in winds as low as 10 knots, so it really doesn't take a big storm.

If winds become gusty while you are kiting, keep your kite low in the wind window (10:00 or 2:00) and get to a safe place. It can be tempting to wait for the gusts to settle down and try and get out for a short time, but remember, gusts can start back up at any time. If the weather is changing, you are at risk of a downturn at any minute with no warning. Do an online search for "kiteboarder lofted," and you will see a lot of video that demonstrates just how sudden and dangerous lofting is. Onshore wind conditions are particularly dangerous when lofting conditions are present because of the chance of being slammed into a hard object.

Serious injuries and even fatalities have resulted from kiters being lofted, and a number of the fatalities have been very experienced riders. It is important to understand that lofting isn't something that you can quit paying attention to when you get more advanced; it happens to the best of us.

Riding Upwind

When you start kiteboarding, you will be doing a lot of walking upwind to get back to where you started from. Among kiteboarders it's called "the walk of shame," but really, it's just part of being a beginner. Frankly, you will have so much fun that you won't mind the walk. After you get your basic skills down, though, it's time to start working on kiting upwind.

The main thing that is going to get you going upwind is your boardwork, but how you position your body and how you use your kite are important too. To begin traveling upwind, you want to position your kite at least 45 to 60 degrees above the horizon.

Keep a straight front leg with your back leg bent; the weight over your back leg and toes can come up so heel digs in. Keep your body long with your hips pushing upwards as you lean back; don't bend at the waist or squat. Rotate your upper body so that your chest faces where you want to go and your face points slightly upwind of the tack you are on. Remember, your head must face direction you want to go.

Going upwind, with a "side-on" shore wind

One-hand grab on surfboard with no footstraps

Another shot of a one-hand grab on a surfboard with no footstraps

Chapter 5 FAQs & Common Misconceptions

Q: Every time I try to stand up on my board I fall on my face. What am I doing wrong?

A: The most likely problem is that you are letting your body move too far forward. It's natural to want to work your legs the same way, but what you need to do on a waterstart is to keep your weight over your rear foot and pull it under you as you start to straighten your front leg.

Wave Riding

Chapter 6: Buying Gear

Finding What Works Best for You

When you take a lesson from a professional instructor, you have access to equipment that has presumably been selected to match your needs and has been maintained appropriately. As mentioned earlier, using the instructor's equipment gives you a good opportunity to try out the gear and see how it works for you.

You may find that a particular set up is difficult for you to maneuver, a harness is too large or small, or a release is too stiff for your fingers or too small for your bear paws to manipulate. Most equipment is intended to work for just about everyone, but what matters is that *your* equipment works for *you*.

If you have a family that will be kiting with you, make sure equipment is fitted to each individual and that everyone can handle all of the equipment that they will be using. It may be tempting to save money by having one family member pay for a lesson and then teach everybody else, but the improved safety of having each person properly instructed is well worth the investment.

New vs. Used Equipment

Unless you are buying from your instructor the equipment that you used in your lessons, be very cautious about used equipment. Don't be shy about testing it out first. Until you have some experience with kiting equipment and know how to recognize signs of wear, stick to buying new equipment or barely used equipment from an instructor who knows its history.

You can get used equipment for a lot less than you pay for new, but the experience can be much like buying a used car. Sure, it's possible that it sat in the garage and only got taken around the block at Christmas, but it could also be used and abused, with internal damage that you won't know about until it fails on you.

Shops vs. Dealers

Make sure that you buy your equipment from a person who is knowledgeable about the sport. General sporting goods stores aim to hire people for each department that have practical experience in their given sport, but unfortunately there's no telling whether a kiter will be on the clock when you're there to shop. You need the expertise of someone with more than just knowledge of the prices on gear.

Many instructors are dealers for one or more preferred manufacturers. An instructor often has a few favorite lines of equipment that they trust to maintain high quality, and this is what they recommend to their students. The advantage of focusing on one or two brands is that the dealer can easily stay abreast of all the latest developments in technology and techniques. However, there are other instructors that choose to offer a greater variety in brands and equipment models. This is great for students that want a variety of choices in different price ranges.

Forums

As you develop into an experienced kiter, you will invariably want to branch out and experiment with different kinds of equipment. Online forums can be a great place to get information about which products other kiters are using and how well the equipment has worked out for them. Most of the time you'll find forum members are helpful to new members, but remember that every forum has a jerk or two. Always be sure you know who you are dealing with before agreeing to any transactions with someone you meet online.

Professional Riders

Not all professionals are instructors, and most are sponsored by a manufacturer. While it is important to remember that their advice may be biased towards a sponsor, they can be a great source of information. They will always keep on top of the latest developments in the field and can give advice for different skill levels.

Conclusion

That wraps up the ground school basics. Nothing can replace getting a kite in your hands and a board under your feet for getting a taste of the real thrill that this sport is about, but there's a lot of information that you need to know in order to kite successfully and safely. I hope this book gives you a solid understanding of the sport and proves useful as a reference in the years to come.

Welcome to the world of kiteboarding; I hope you enjoy it as much as I do! Whatever your taste for adventure may be – zipping along the coastline, cruising a lake, snowkiting across mountain passes and frozen lakes, or even traversing sandy beaches on a land board – kiting is a great way to enjoy the outdoors and is a fun addition to an active lifestyle.

Team rider Bonetti living the Kite Life in La Ventana, Mexico

Acknowledgements

Many thanks to "Wainman Hawaii"® for the use of their User Manual and photographs.

International kiteboarding instructor, Tyson Sullivan, reviewed the book and provided some helpful tips in addition to a few suggested revisions. I am grateful for his help and commitment to keeping our sport safe.

A sincere thank you to Jon Bonetti and Deidra Lewis (TheRealBonetti.com) for sharing the kiteboarding lifestyle through their photographs.

Tanja Kopper's photography ([Tanja Kopper | Photography](#)) captures the power and beauty of kitesurfing, and I appreciate her allowing me to use her photos.

Thanks to my team at Kite Surf North America. I appreciate all the support.

I am also very appreciative of the support I received from the staff of Content Divas. Their expertise in editing, formatting, press releases, and online marketing has made writing and publishing my first book amazingly simple.

I personally would like to thank you for downloading and reading this book. "Thank You!" While it is impossible to include everything there is to know about Kitesurfing in one edition, we do hope that you've found this to be a benefit to your learning how to kitesurf. Be Safe and Have Fun!

About the Author

    Shawn Tieskotter is a dedicated outdoorsman who has shared his passion for life in all 50 states and 25 other countries. From lobstering in Maine to cruising the beaches of Baja and from ice-climbing in the Swiss Alps to hang-gliding in Brazil and scuba diving Honduras, Shawn has truly experienced the thrill and wonder that can only be found in nature.

    Shawn's quest to experience as many of the Earth's wonders as possible has led him on a 3-day camel trip in the Sahara Desert, a 4-month camping trip in Alaska, and even a drive through Canada to the Arctic Circle. In addition to hiking the highest peak in North Africa, he spent a summer in his home state, Colorado, hiking 20 of the Rocky Mountains' 12-14,000 foot peaks. Not being limited to physical conquests, Shawn studied Spanish in Costa Rica and Guatemala.

    Currently, Shawn's greatest outdoor passion is kiteboarding, which he considers to be the pinnacle of outdoor sports. Though his search for the perfect activity is over, he continues to search for the best spots and the friendliest people on the planet to pursue and share his passion for kiting with.

    His boundless enthusiasm for the sport drove Shawn to get involved in efforts to make the sport as safe as it can be and accessible to as many people as possible by becoming a kiting instructor. Since he couldn't find a book that fully covered the sport and gave new kiters all the information they needed to get a safe and successful start in the sport, he decided to write one himself.

In writing this book, it is his hope that you will find the sport of kiting just as exciting and rewarding as he does, and that you share his commitment to safety.

Contributor: Tyson Sullivan

Tyson's love affair with board sports began when he was introduced to snowboarding at the age of nine. Growing up in the Pacific Northwest, he did everything in his power to get as much time on the mountain as possible.

The affair took a dazzling turn in 2004, when he discovered kiteboarding while on vacation in Maui. He knew he had to try it, but had no idea it would become the driving force in his life for the next 10 years (and counting). He was hooked from the first lesson, and by the spring of 2007 he had earned his Professional Air Sports Association (PASA) instructors certification and became a full time instructor for Urbansurf, the largest kiteboarding school in the state of Washington.

When winter came, Tyson headed south, and became an instructor for Miami Kiteboarding, one of the largest schools in the country, where he received his International Kiteboarding Organization (IKO) instructor certification. In addition to four seasons as a kiteboarding instructor in South Florida and three seasons teaching in Cape Cod, Massachusetts, he has also been a snowkiting instructor in Dillon, CO.

Tyson's years of experience in a wide variety of environments and with several brands of equipment have made him a very versatile instructor and rider. His passion for kiting hasn't waned, and he is enthusiastic about training new kiters so they can safely experience the sport that has been so fulfilling for him.

Get Started Today!

HowToKitesurf.com

www.ingramcontent.com/pod-product-compliance
Lightning Source LLC
Chambersburg PA
CBHW041659160426
43191CB00002B/29